TURNING OVER

For Patrick Taggart

BRIAN THOMPSON

TURNING OVER

AMBER LANE PRESS

First published in 1984 by
Amber Lane Press Ltd
9 Middle Way
Oxford OX2 7LH

Printed in Great Britain by
Cotswold Press Ltd, Oxford

Copyright © Brian Thompson, 1984

ISBN 0 906399 56 4

CONDITIONS OF SALE

Turning Over was first presented at the Bush Theatre, London, on 9th December, 1983. It was directed by David Hayman, with the following cast:

FRANK .... Charles Dance
MEHTA .... Nadim Sawalha
MARTIN .... Gary Waldhorn
KEITH .... Peter Jonfield
CHRIS .... David Sibley
SALLY .... Geraldine James
PENNY .... Frances Barber

Decor: Sue Plummer
Lighting: Gerry Jenkinson
Sound: Steve Emms

CHARACTERS

FRANK
MEHTA
MARTIN
KEITH
CHRIS
SALLY
PENNY

The stage is divided into upper and lower. On the lower stage is a cutting room, with a practical Steenbeck and three chairs.

On the upper stage is 'India': that is, scenes from the film that is being edited. The only stage furniture necessary, however, is two or three white rattan chairs.

ACT ONE

FRANK *is leaning against the Steenbeck. He is staring at the screen. He checks over aloud the elements of the film.*

FRANK: We can get *on* the train but we can't get off. Okay. We've got the hotel, triff, we've got the gardener, the old guy with the beard, we've got the wedding, the water-buffalo, the kid with the sores, the other kid with the teeshirt, we've got the wedding, no I've said the wedding, we've got…we've got the river crossing, the interview with the girl, the piece in the church, his bit to camera about the garden…we've got the temple, which is useless.

> [*He thinks long and hard.*]

[*in agony*] Oh, *God.*

The lights go down on FRANK, *and the upper stage is lit.*

MR MEHTA *is sitting on one of the chairs, in slacks and a nylon shirt. He is middle-aged and anxious. He clutches a worn brief-case to him. He sees an invisible someone approach, takes his spectacles from his shirt pocket and puts them on. He rises politely. The someone he is there to meet is* FRANK.

FRANK: Mr Mehta?
MEHTA: Welcome to our city. Welcome to our country. Welcome. B.A. Mehta, BA Tourism. My business card.
FRANK: [*reads*] B.A. Mehta…BA Tourims. Triff.
MEHTA: [*stiff*] This word is tourism.
FRANK: It says tourims.

> [MEHTA *examines the card carefully. He is displeased.*
> *He smiles sadly.*]

MEHTA: For this I am blaming my brother-in-law.
FRANK: Anyway, nice to meet you and thanks for coming. I —
MEHTA: You are old friend of India?
FRANK: No. What it was about was, I wondered if —
MEHTA: May I tell you something straight away? The bus you

have been hiring to carry your team here and there in this most beautiful spot on earth belongs to a very bad man.

FRANK: Also called Mehta.

MEHTA: My cousin. You find him an ignorant fellow? He is ignorant. What he understands only is the internal combustion engine. We have laughed about this.

FRANK: Who have? You and your cousin?

MEHTA: No, no, no. Myself and my touristical associates. Professor Anantramia...from Madras...a very learned man. Please. You will smoke?

FRANK: Just put one out. Now look, Mr Mehta, as you know we are making a film —

MEHTA: [*correcting him, primly*] — shooting —

FRANK: — yes, shooting. And our presenter is an Englishman called Martin Fuller, who's um, a writer, and —

MEHTA: A very intelligent fellow. I have seen him. He wears a nice suiting, I would say from Bond Street, England. Would I be correct there?

FRANK: On the button. Good. Great. So anyway...we'd like to shoot a sequence with you and Mr Fuller, in which you talk together, you know, informally, about this hill station and its history, and stuff like that. Just one little sequence in the film. You know.

> [MEHTA *takes off his glasses with an elaborate gesture and looks judicious.*]

MEHTA: This...may be possible.

FRANK: Great! Well now —

MEHTA: But! First, we must ask ourselves, what details should be included in this film? What purpose is it having? We can take for example the Church of St. Stephen, built in eighteen hundred thirty four by the Scottish MacaNulty, after the plan of a similar edifice in Dumfries, for which I have excellent postcard.

FRANK: Yeah, well —

MEHTA: — Second!

> [*He wags a finger at* FRANK.]

Ev-ery-bod-y that comes here must of course dwell

with satisfaction on the story of the railway, which was completed by an Italian firm, British rolling stock, eighteen hundred and eight one, at a cost of half a million rupees…in *modern* money this would be — you guess, please!

FRANK: The idea is that you sit down with Martin — Mr Fuller — and just chat. Nothing special. Just chat. Chinwag.

    [MEHTA *stares.*]

MEHTA: Chinwag. Yes. Here, please.

    [*He hands over a second card.* FRANK *reads.*]

FRANK: Mountain Joy Rides.

MEHTA: Buses, coaches, taxis. Experienced driver, my personal services on all itineraries, English-style packed lunch if required.

FRANK: Shan't need it. Not necessary. It's just an interview. Chat.

MEHTA: Chinwag.

FRANK: Exactly.

    [MEHTA *smiles sadly. He is very disappointed.*]

MEHTA: You are perhaps aware of Mr Alan Whicker from your country.

FRANK: Yep.

MEHTA: A good friend.

FRANK: He hired you.

MEHTA: Mr Rooney: Production Unit Manager. Mr Sharples, cameraman. Ted and Bazzer. Miss um…Barbara.

FRANK: Triff.

    [*He looks up.* MARTIN *enters. He is in his new safari suit with the short sleeves.*]

Martin, this is Mr Mehta. He's a friend of Alan Vickers. I'll leave you two to discuss what you're going to say. I'll get the crew.

MARTIN: How do you do Mr Mehta? How nice to meet you. Frank's been telling you a little about our film, has he? I think I met Mr Vicar yesterday. From Southampton. The crane driver for the French construction company. Very amusing man. I suppose he's shown you his tattoos? They —

MEHTA: No. That is Mr Vicar. I am talking about Mr Alan
         Whicker.
MARTIN: Alan…? Oh, I see. 'High on a hill, hurled higgledy-
         piggledy from the haughty Himalayas, history…
         happily…
                 [*He is running out of H's.* MEHTA *passes him a card.*]
         Mountain Joy Rides.
MEHTA: Church, railway station, old dam, new dam, old town,
         new town, sacred hill, very old temple, silver-smithy
         — [*He leans in.*] — you play chess?
MARTIN: I try to, occasionally, I —
MEHTA: I make you very good price for inlay chess set. Ivory
         and jade pieces, traditional Indian design. This is
         possible. Also sari for wife. You are distinguished
         author?
MARTIN: Yes. But a divorced distinguished author.
MEHTA: Very sad. Tell me, please: what is subject of this film?
MARTIN: Contentment.
MEHTA: Yes? Please?
MARTIN: What do you think? You think it's a good idea?
MEHTA: This word is not known to me.
MARTIN: You mean…? I see. Yes, point taken. Well, it's not
         political.
                 [*Now* MEHTA *is foxed.*]
MEHTA: What?
MARTIN: Not a political film.
MEHTA: A political film is not possible.
MARTIN: Indeed not. More's the pity.
MEHTA: Ah! You think so?
MARTIN: In some ways, yes. It is a pity.
MEHTA: For this kind of film you are needing permissions from
         Prime Minister, Foreign Affairs, Internal Affairs and
         India High Commission. Which they will not give.
MARTIN: As I say, however, this isn't the film we are making.
MEHTA: Then please. Expound. I am listening with all ears.
MARTIN: Well, we've only just…it's um…the subject is the
         sense of contentment to be got from place. I mean the
         series is called 'I Could Be Happy Here', um?

MEHTA: You are happy here?

MARTIN: That's just the series title. But the underlying theme, I
           would say, comes from exploring...oneself...finding
           oneself...at peace perhaps...among splendid sur-
           roundings such as this. The sense of joy that comes —
           I think it comes over each and every one of us — it can
           come — when we...You don't think it's a very good
           idea?

MEHTA: This is film for cinema?

MARTIN: For television.

               [MEHTA's *mind clears.*]

MEHTA: Ah! University Challenge! Master Mind. Call my
           Bluff!

MARTIN: That's it.

MEHTA: What you are doing is just entertainment?

MARTIN: More and more do I realise that. [*He glances.*] Who is
           that girl?

MEHTA: [*peers*] That is Mrs S.S. Seshu Aiyar.

MARTIN: No, not her. The European girl she's talking to.

MEHTA: Ah. She is married to one of the scientists up at the
           tracking station. I think. Or maybe she is a hippy.

MARTIN: You think so?

MEHTA: I do not know this one.

               [KEITH, *the sound recordist, walks on. He is in the hot-
               weather gear of film crews — Rocky Horror teeshirt
               and baggy shorts, floppy hat and nagra.*]

KEITH: Frank sent me. There's going to be a delay. Rodge has
           got the squits. How are *you*?

MARTIN: Perfectly okay.

KEITH: There's nothing left in me but water. What a country.
           Who's the bird?

MARTIN: We don't know.

KEITH: [*unexcited*] Things could be looking up.
               [*Blackout.*]

In the cutting room: CHRIS *has joined* FRANK.

CHRIS: No, wait a minute. Wait a minute. You got the kid

with the sores, you got the old guy with the beard…
you got the cement factory…

FRANK: Are you kidding?

CHRIS: You shot it. What about Mehta's temple-bashing?

FRANK: Oh God. I should have chucked old Tourims into the
cement works. No, it's got to be the interview with the
girl.

CHRIS: Yeah, but Frank —

FRANK: All right. He comes into the room; before he even sits
down we cut away, you know, bam, back to her, she's
talking, yap yap, his noddies…

CHRIS: Cut away to what?

FRANK: I don't know. How do I know? There's the big close up
of the table and the flowers and the wine-glass –

CHRIS: — and in the two shot later, someone's taken the flowers
off the table.

FRANK: [*defeated*] Yeah.

CHRIS: Who did that?

FRANK: I don't know. [*He laughs.*] It was hot out there, man.
It's a hot country. You start going bismarck.

CHRIS: My son the director!
                    [FRANK *laughs.*]

FRANK: I'm telling you. It's all right for you, but it's a hot
country. *He* was being difficult…the cameraman
wouldn't work without his own brand of iced drinks,
that you could only buy at the station — you had to
send down to the station in a cab for Rodge's drinks —
two dozen Orange Gold — it was *hot*.

CHRIS: You were stoned.

FRANK: I was stoned. No, I wasn't stoned.

CHRIS: No?

FRANK: I can't remember. I'm stoned now. Chris, Chris, what
are we going to *do*?

CHRIS: See what he says. What time's he coming?

FRANK: Three. I offered him lunch; he wouldn't have it.

CHRIS: Perhaps he knows what you feel about him.

FRANK: Yeah. How about this, then, wait a minute: we drop

the interview altogether, go straight to the seaside…
the ocean…the sea…the seascape…the *sunset.*

CHRIS: Not another sunset. You can't. You can't. You can't
drop his interview.

FRANK: He won't mind.

CHRIS: Can't do it.

FRANK: He won't notice.

CHRIS: Everyone else will. The film will only run —

> [*He consults a grease pencil tally on the bed of his
> Steenbeck.*]

— fifty four fifty.

FRANK: Plus titles.

CHRIS: That's with titles.

FRANK: [*incredulous*] Fifty four fifty.

CHRIS: That's with very long titles.

FRANK: Oh my God.

> [*They ponder; the lights stay up on the cutting room, but
> CHRIS has punched the start button on the machine, so at
> the same time the light goes up in 'India'. MARTIN is
> giving his sum-up of the experience. He starts in sound,
> but CHRIS wants to think, so he drops the level and
> MARTIN continues in mute. He is walking and pointing,
> smiling and performing, but in dumb-show.*]

MARTIN: 'So finally, what is the experience of this place? What
lessons can one learn — can one be happy here? The
answer is, I think, surprising. To begin with —'

> [*He goes into dumb-show as CHRIS puts the sound down
> with the toe of his shoe. At a certain point, MARTIN
> freezes. Then CHRIS switches him off and the light goes
> out in 'India'.*]

FRANK: Okay. This then. We drop the interview — no, wait a
minute — we drop the int. and put back —

FRANK:
CHRIS: } [*together*] The water-buffalo!

> [*They burst into hysterical laughter and fall about.
> CHRIS gives us his buffalo imitation.*]

CHRIS: Horunk! Horunn-k!

> [*But the renewed laughter subsides. They fall silent again.*]

CHRIS: I'm not thrilled about the *first* sunset, either.

FRANK: *Great* sunset.

CHRIS: Too obvious.

FRANK: They are. That's the nature of them.

CHRIS: Yawn, yawn.

FRANK: They're good television.

CHRIS: Write that down.

FRANK: [*despairing*] Oh bloody hell…No sunset, no interview, the sequence where he takes the ferry across the river is…No! I'm not going to drop the sunset. [*He reflects moodily.*] Drop the wedding if you like.

CHRIS: The wedding's great.

FRANK: It would be, if he wasn't in every shot. What a nit.

CHRIS: Anybody can get stung on the end of the nose.

FRANK: But not everybody thinks of putting a Bandaid on it when they're slipping unobtrusively through an Indian wedding. He got more attention than the bride.

CHRIS: [*exasperated*] Yesterday —

FRANK: I know what I said yesterday. No. Look. Go back to the int. What else have we got? In the interview? What else have we got? Can we come to it late, when he's already there?

CHRIS: What about the big wide angle?

FRANK: Terrible. No. I got it! What about…?

> [*But the thought evaporates.* CHRIS *yawns.*]

Exactly.

CHRIS: She looks nice, the girl. Did you have her?

FRANK: Did *I* have her?

CHRIS: Your type.

FRANK: Definitely not my type.

CHRIS: Who found her?

FRANK: He did. Old Scaramouche.

CHRIS: So he had her?

FRANK: The mind, possibly. A heavy lady.

CHRIS: Her mind doesn't look like her best bit, bits.

FRANK: Triff. If he hears you say that we'll have another row.

CHRIS: You forgot. He likes me. Ah-ah! Didn't realise that, did you?

FRANK: And why do you think that is? It's because you're a machine operator, matey. They like all that. If you were a train driver, he'd like you. Well, not a train driver. But a bus conductor. Put up the cement works, then.

CHRIS: It was just a suggestion.

FRANK: Anything.

> [*Their lights go down.*]

MEHTA, *very formal, and* MARTIN *are on camera. They are out of doors, in front of the cement works. The table and chairs have been struck.* MEHTA*'s gestures are large.*

MEHTA: And all this cement works was built originally for the erection of the very important tracking station and observatory, erected, or shall we say constructed, nineteen hundred seventy three, at a cost of many millions of rupees.

> [*He lowers his voice apologetically and catches* MARTIN *in his noddies.*]

I do not know exactly how many rupees but this I can find out.

> [MARTIN *ignores that and says, loud, for camera:*]

MARTIN: So what you're saying is that all this was built for the construction of the observatory?

> [MEHTA *is confused.*]

MEHTA: Yes, I have just said.

> [MARTIN *ploughs on.*]

MARTIN: And tell me this, then —

FRANK: [*off*] Cut!

> [FRANK *storms on.*]

[*to* MEHTA] What are you trying to do? You're trying to sell a cement works that doesn't belong to you? What is this, a cement work saga? [*turning to* MARTIN] And you. Are you going to repeat everything he says? You *touch* the cement works, just *touch* it. I only…I only

want the smoke and the faces of the labourers up to their eyeballs in it. I mean you're just here. You're — okay. Okay. Don't say anything. Don't – we'll shoot it tight and wide, but don't speak. You just...happen to be taking a stroll past the — Rodge!
> [*He calls the invisible* RODGE.]
Rodge, you stay put. You — I don't *care*.
> [*He seizes* MEHTA *by the shoulders and spins him to face upstage.*]
You see that smoke? That's what I make films out of. Smoke.

MEHTA: This is so?

FRANK: This is so. Now we're going to go again and all I want you to do is stand there. [*shouting to* RODGE] It's a mute, we'll end board it. Okay Martin. Just stand there. Turn over.
> [*He leaves them. They glance out of the corner of their eyes. They sense the camera running. They are stiffened by fear. Suddenly,* MARTIN *is doubled over.*]

MARTIN: Argh!

FRANK: [*off*] Oh, bloody hell, what now?

MARTIN: Bitten, by a — godalmighty, was it a bird?

MEHTA: It was a fly. A big fly.
> [FRANK *walks on. He speaks with exaggerated calm.*]

FRANK: Rodge has just gone to change his shorts.

MARTIN: I have been bitten by an enormous fly.

FRANK: [*calm*] So I saw. Terriff.
> [*He walks off.*]

MEHTA: These flies. You know they are very bad at this time of year. Sometimes they will kill horses. You would like to meet the Cement Works Manager, Mr Desai?

MARTIN: Bandaid. In my jacket pocket.
> [MEHTA *shyly puts his hand in* MARTIN'*s pocket. He discovers a pakora.*]

MEHTA: You have not eaten your pakora?

MARTIN: No, I — you have it.
> [MEHTA *munches.* MARTIN *fixes his Bandaid.*]

MEHTA: I will say this. If you make films from smoke, this
          cement works is a very good place for shooting…
MARTIN: I am going to kill Frank.
MEHTA: Kill Frank?
MARTIN: Wouldn't you like to?
MEHTA: I am — on this one I am ambi-valent.
MARTIN: Ambivalent.
MEHTA: Yes.
          [*Blackout.*]

*Lights up on the cutting room. The viewing of the cement work
sequence hasn't improved morale.*

CHRIS: You'd think he'd have more glamour. Writing books
          and all that.
FRANK: You've been stuck in here too long.
CHRIS: Writes books.
FRANK: Plays golf, collects W.H. Bleeding Auden, did his
          National Service in Kenya, triff, but can't think. He
          can think, but he can't — what's the word I want? I
          dunno. He's un-nimble. How long could you let that
          smoke run?
CHRIS: [*dismayed*] It's just smoke, Frank-ee.
FRANK: Yeah. Okay. We're going to use the interview.
CHRIS: [*warns*] It won't cut.
FRANK: Well, every picture has its little dull moment, we'll cut
          it the best way we can. She's nice. She's got nice legs…
          her *legs*! There's a cutaway we could use, a shot — she
          shows her legs, dead elegant.
CHRIS: It's not in the film.
FRANK: It's not? That's the trouble. You forget what is, and
          what isn't.
CHRIS: What'd he say?
FRANK: What about?
CHRIS: Didn't he have any feelings, about working with you?
FRANK: How do I know? Just two grammar school boys,
          twenty years apart. What was he supposed to say?
CHRIS: It was the same grammar school.

FRANK: Oh yeah. He mentioned it. He writes bits about it. He wrote a bit about some tennis courts on the Great Cambridge Road — 'A North London Childhood' for the *Guardian*. Where he used to go as a kid. Some toffee like that. Big Tory country. I showed it to my mother. Yes, she said, and not a word about Arsenal. That was your undoing, she said. The old man was Spurs down to his socks. So is Martin, of course. Naturally. Yeah. Jubilee Park. He could just remember it. That's where *we* played tennis. But it wasn't quite leafy enough for Martin. Good luck to him. All I want is a film that runs to length. And a holiday. And a divorce.

CHRIS: He's beaten you there.

FRANK: Not by much.
            [*Lights down.*]

Lights up in 'India'. MARTIN *is rehearsing his lines. He has a larger Bandaid on the end of his nose. His voice is low. It is morning, and he is trying out some ideas that may have come to him at dawn, in a sorry attempt to bridge the gap between himself and* FRANK...*When* FRANK *enters he is as flat as a steel plate.*

MARTIN: 'The, ah, light that falls in India is so bright that it obscures rather than revealing. Down there on the plain, there is a shade temperature of a hundred and —' oh, Frank.

FRANK: I'm cabbaged.

MARTIN: The Glen Fiddich. Gave it a bit of a hammering last night.

FRANK: That and the finest Lebanese gold.

MARTIN: It's a wonder how it gets down here. We're — we must be two thousand miles from Lebanon.

FRANK: I bought it in Shepherd's Bush, is the answer to that. That's the size of this film. I'm importing dope to India.

MARTIN: I was just thinking about a little piece of light.

FRANK: The light.

MARTIN: You know.
    [*He waves his arms about.*]
FRANK: [*sour*] Triff.
MARTIN: You don't like it?
FRANK: Like what?
MARTIN: The idea.
FRANK: *Things*, Martin. I film things.
    [*Enter* MEHTA *and* KEITH, *ambling.* MEHTA *is patiently waiting on the foreign court of princes. To pass the time he is telling* KEITH *a joke.* KEITH *is impassive.*]
MEHTA: ...and that man said, this is not one bicycle but two bicycle!
    [*He laughs.* KEITH *stares.*]
KEITH: Is that it? That's the punchline is it?
MEHTA: [*giggling*] Yes. This is a very new joke.
KEITH: Bicycle joke.
MEHTA: Yes, yes, bicycle.
FRANK: [*dour*] Morning.
MEHTA: The sacred hill?
FRANK: Nope.
MEHTA: But yesterday you said —
FRANK: [*to* KEITH] Where's Rodge?
KEITH: 'S'just shoving on some bum ointment. Any news of Annette?
FRANK: Up on that hill, Keith, they've got — right behind the cement works there — they've got the third world's finest tracking station and observatory, mate. I mean, if a bolt pries loose on a satellite, or someone flushes the toilet on the Soyuz 7, they can pick that up, while, at the same time, peering into the ultimate mysteries of space and time. At the touch of a button, a pile sufferer in that place can speak by satellite to a fellow sufferer in Washington, and have his message relaycd in the twinkle of an eye to Woomera, Hawaii, or anywhere else you like. But what they haven't got is a phone line to Bombay. I don't *know* how Annette is. We're going to film here this morning.
KEITH: Yeah?

FRANK: Martin's bit to camera.

MARTIN: [*alarmed*] My — which bit?

MEHTA: You're not going to the sacred hill?

FRANK: Er, no. Now look, B.A., down in Bombay, is a big fat jolly girl who is the production assistant to this little epic. She stayed behind to look after the sparks, right? Bernard. Who is ill. With the Shits. At the time it seemed a good idea for Annettypoos to see him through his little crisis. What I would like you to do is to use your considerable influence to phone Bombay — no wait a minute — to find *some* way of getting in touch with the Taj, Bombay, and find out what's keeping Annette. Now. Here is a London number. You ring that, they ring Bombay, then they ring you back. Is possible? Or you can ring Shanghai if you like; or send a runner.

MARTIN: What about the railway telegraph?

FRANK: Brill. Good boy. Try that.

MEHTA: [*uncertain*] Mr Frank…

FRANK: Shooting, B.A., shooting. Off you go. All right, Martin, do it here. Um…just…

> [MARTIN *picks up a chair tentatively.*]

Good. All right, Rodge! Right, Keith. Turn over.

MARTIN: But Frank!

KEITH: Running.

FRANK: First ideas are best ideas, Martin.

> [*He holds up the slate.*]

Going to use the chair?

> [MARTIN *straddles it, Hollywood fashion.* KEITH *kneels and leans in.* FRANK *marks the slate.*]

Disaster Productions, slate three six, take one.

> [*He claps the board.*]

Give it a minute.

> [*He walks off.* MARTIN *is exposed…*]

MARTIN: 'Everybody's…' [*He coughs.*] Sorry.

FRANK: [*off*] Keep running.

MARTIN: Frog in the throat. 'Everybody's idea of a hill station is, say, a chunk of Surrey put down in the middle of nowhere, or rather up a mountain...' Sod it. Keep running.

FRANK: [*off*] Take your time. Camera's running.

MARTIN: 'You know, people think of hill stations as the places where the colonels and their ladies retreated in the hottest of weathers, to dream of England; and so it...' Just a minute.

FRANK: [*off*] Cut. Hang on, Martin.

> [KEITH *walks on, in preposterous shorts and a floppy hat. He kneels in front of* MARTIN *and adjusts his mike, which should be taped to his chest but has slipped down.*]

KEITH: Look at my bloody arms! Peeled raw.

MARTIN: [*low*] What do you think?

KEITH: [*absently*] What about?

MARTIN: Do you think it's all right?

KEITH: No. Can't hear you.

MARTIN: I can feel it slipping down. That's why I stopped. The tape won't stick to my skin.

KEITH: Would do if you had hairs on your chest.

> [FRANK *walks in. He is professionally encouraging, that is to say non-committal.*]

FRANK: Great. Looks nice. Just relax.

MARTIN: Bit um —

FRANK: Don't worry about that. There's a full mag on. Keep the 'you know' bit going.

MARTIN: What bit was that?

FRANK: The bit where you say 'you know.' You know. Loose. Free. [*Pause.*] Do you *want* to sit like that?

MARTIN: Like what?

KEITH: Like Montgomery Clift.

FRANK: Let's go again.

> [*He marks the board with the take number.*]

Wait a minute. What slate number are we?

> [*He wanders away.*]

MARTIN: [*calls*] Frank? Do I look like Montgomery Clift?

> [*A long silence.*]

FRANK: [*off*] Should you?

MARTIN: *Keith* —

KEITH: [*with irony*] Ta.

        [FRANK *walks back in.*]

FRANK: C'mon, Keith.

        [*He looks towards the invisible* RODGE. KEITH *holds the mike in towards the board.*]

        Thirty six, take two.

        [*He and* KEITH *leave.* MARTIN *waits. He strokes his hair swiftly, nods abruptly, then, just as abruptly begins:*]

MARTIN: 'People think of these hill stations as the places where the colonels and their ladies retreated out of exasperation with the heat and dust, and so it was once. But those ghosts have long been exorcised.'

        [*He rises and puts a foot on the chair. At the same instant the light goes up in the cutting room.*]

CHRIS: What?

FRANK: Run him back.

        [*Both lights are up.* MARTIN *'runs' backwards, speaking backwards — he sits on the chair, talks backwards, nods, strokes his hair. Then he runs forwards again, giving the same lines at breakneck speed, rises from the chair...and plumps down again...rises and plumps down.*]

FRANK: When does he put his hand on the chair to get up?

CHRIS: Clean. No problems.

FRANK: Okay, run on. There's a better take.

        [*So* MARTIN *takes his foot off the chair and walks to the verandah; suddenly spurts as* CHRIS *pushes the fast forward button, is back at his mark;* KEITH *walks in, touches his chest to check the mike; the sequence starts again...it's a fluff...* KEITH *walks in...* MARTIN *starts again...all this in double time. He gets up from the chair, walks to the verandah and* now *we are at voice speed:*]

MARTIN: 'What the British did, with the inadvertence of all great empires, the inadvertence that all great empires must show, was to create conditions that would outlast them.' And my microphone is down by my belly button.

FRANK: [*off*] Cut!

> [KEITH *saunters on.*]

KEITH: You must have breasts like a woman's.

> [MARTIN *ignores him.*]

MARTIN: Frank! I am getting just a little bit confused.

FRANK: [*off*] Just hang on a tick.

KEITH: 'Inadvertence?'

MARTIN: What about it?

FRANK: [*off*] Okay, Martin, pick up where you are. Just turn your head. The other way. Maybe…put your hand in your pocket…?

MARTIN: No *thank* you.

FRANK: Yeah, yeah. You're right. Keith! Turn over, we'll end board it.

> [KEITH *moves back, leaving* MARTIN *alone, exposed.*]

MARTIN: Frank? I'm very sorry about this.

FRANK: [*off*] That's all right.

MARTIN: It is…enormously difficult to pursue a train of thought when —

FRANK: [*off*] That's *okay.*

MARTIN: I thought I'd like to clear that up with —

FRANK: [*off, bellows*] Only we are still *running.*

MARTIN: Of course! Right! Oh, God…

> [*He thinks for a moment.*]

'You see, it comes down to this. What the British left, at least in this particular place, the thing that's so commonly taken to be a legacy of class and snobbery, is actually something much more alive, a hundred-year-old garden, in fact, of trees as well as plants and shrubs, lakes, even architectural follies. When you look out there, you see really no more than a large and lovingly constructed garden…'

> [*He is suddenly rapt. He studies the view and adds slowly:*]

'That I would dearly love to enter.'

FRANK: [*off*] And out! Triff! Check the gate.
              [KEITH *wanders in.*]
KEITH: You make that up as you went along?
MARTIN: It showed, did it?
KEITH: I'm just interested.
MARTIN: [*touched*] Thank you, Keith.
KEITH: So what did it mean?
MARTIN: [*bitter*] Thanks. What happened here, a long time ago, yesterday by Indian standards, they cut back the jungle, burned it off — I don't know what — and then they sent back to England for seeds and saplings, and bits of architectural style they saw in builders' catalogues. They carried everything up that mountain out there, Keith, and they quite accidentally made a work of art. That would outlast them. Until the cows come home. That was grace, and harmony.
KEITH: Why didn't you say that?
MARTIN: [*deflated*] Why didn't I?
KEITH: Don't get me wrong. It was good sound in the end. No problems there.
MARTIN: Fine.
KEITH: It's just I thought you was going to say what we're doing here.
MARTIN: Exactly.
KEITH: Ne'er mind, eh?
MARTIN: No. Never mind.
KEITH: [*going*] Rodge has got the shits something chronic. It's all this bleeding curry...
              [MARTIN *looks round him disconsolately. He reaches in his pocket and finds his notes. He reads them and grimaces. He catches someone's eye* — SALLY*'s* — *his first meeting with her.*]
MARTIN: Hello.
SALLY: Hi.
MARTIN: Come and keep me company.
              [SALLY *walks on in a long-sleeved cotton robe, belt and little purse, bare legs, sandals.*]
We're um, shooting a film.

SALLY: I realise.

MARTIN: I didn't see you earlier when I was — you weren't watching when —?

SALLY: When what?

MARTIN: Thank God for that. I'm Martin Fuller.
    [They shake hands.]

SALLY: Sally Dove. What did you say your name was?

MARTIN: Fuller.

SALLY: BBC?

MARTIN: I'm afraid so. *[hastily]* Not me, but them, yes. That looks cool. Are you at an ashram or something?
    [She ignores the question.]

SALLY: What's your film about?

MARTIN: Well…in London, it's about balance.

SALLY: A documentary?

MARTIN: Yes.

SALLY: Medical?

MARTIN: Sorry?

SALLY: The inner ear.

MARTIN: Ah. No. Balance. Contentment if you like.

SALLY: Where have they all gone?

MARTIN: I wish I knew. Shall we sit down? They disappear like this quite frequently. The bastards.
    [They sit. He is interested in her. She knows it.]

SALLY: You were saying — contentment.

MARTIN: That's how it was explained to me in London. It's a series. If I say Denis Duvallier…?

SALLY: *[polite]* Yes?

MARTIN: I see. No, well, what happened was that he rang me up and said they were thinking of coming out here as part of a series. So we met — lunch — this word balance came into it, which was attractive —

SALLY: You have plenty, do you? Plenty of balance?

MARTIN: None. None at all. But I didn't know that then, you see. Are you on holiday?

SALLY: I live here.

MARTIN: Live here?

SALLY: Yes.

MARTIN: I see. I'm a writer by the way.

SALLY: Not a weights and measures inspector.

MARTIN: Um? No, I meant not a — this is not what I normally do. This. Filming.

SALLY: You're a novelist.

MARTIN: Yes. In a way.

SALLY: I see.

MARTIN: This is the first television I've ever done. [*hesitant, glum*]…I'm a children's writer.

SALLY: Are you an expert on India?

MARTIN: Oh God, if only it worked like that. I met this man at a party — Denis — and a couple of days later he rang me up. For lunch.

SALLY: Why do you write for children?

MARTIN: It's a question I'm often asked. But never, do you see, by children.

> [*She seems not to be embarrassed by his embarrassment.*]

SALLY: That's my house, down there.

> [*She points out over the verandah of the hotel.*]

See the big building? That's the old Fire Station. See that red tin roof to the side of it, a bit higher up the hill? That's my house.

MARTIN: With the tree.

SALLY: With the tree. With the yellow bedsheet hanging out of the window.

MARTIN: That's a bedsheet, is it?

SALLY: You're staying here? This hotel?

MARTIN: Not this one, the other one. This one's got the nicer views. But the crew won't stay here. The other one's got English cuisine.

SALLY: I didn't know that.

MARTIN: Egg and chips. Tomato, egg and chips; chicken and chips; chicken and chips with curried sauce; omelette and chips. Um…corned beef and chips. We brought our own corned beef, in fact, I imagine we paid excess baggage on it. Keith likes it. Do you…live alone?

SALLY: What do *you* eat, then?

MARTIN: There's no point in being dishonest. I had corned beef last night. You don't like answering questions very much, do you? Were you born here perhaps? You're very brown.

SALLY: Leamington. Where else have you been?

MARTIN: [*gloomy*] That's just it. Nowhere. We were whisked straight here by train. I must say I hate railways. Have you any idea of the cost of a fare from King's Cross to York these days?

SALLY: How much? Your right arm?

MARTIN: Your right arm and I've been away a week so it's probably gone up — your right arm and a kidney, or your spleen duct. You can go to Paris cheaper. [*glances*] My daughter's at York. She's studying music. They have an anacoustic chamber there. You can get off the train and go in and listen to your blood boil. D'you miss England?

SALLY: Yes.

MARTIN: You do?

SALLY: It's not so surprising. Do you?

MARTIN: Fervently. Achingly. We left last Monday. Have you ever done any filming? None of them read books. Keith can't read. Frank — Frank is the Director — Frank went to a Polytechnic so far as I can discover.

SALLY: So did I.

MARTIN: Ah yes, but — did you really? I think Frank did philosophy and fairisle pullovers. He failed the philosophy.

SALLY: Is he a good Director?

[*He looks dejectedly at her.*]

MARTIN: Do you know I haven't the faintest idea of how to test the question? Rodge, the cameraman, reads something called *The Dicemen*. There's an electrician we left behind in Bombay. Bernard. They have a drug they're given to stop them up in the event of, you know, the squits. Bernard — the electrician — overdosed as far as I can make out. He's probably exploded by now.

[*She smiles and moves away.*]

You think I'm making it up.

SALLY: So. [*She turns.*] What do you want to happen now?
          [*What he might say in reply is cut short by the arrival of*
          PENNY, *the new producer's assistant. She is lugging a
          suitcase by its strap, has on a badly rumpled teeshirt and
          skirt, bare legs and sandals, but her Sony Walkman is in
          perfect working order.*]
PENNY: Hello, am I late?
          [FRANK *follows her on. He is shaking his head in
          bemusement. The others are confused, stunned.*]
FRANK: Isn't it wonderful? This is Penny Arbagath, who's
          come all the way from London —
PENNY: — Bristol —
FRANK: — as a replacement for Annette, who managed to get
          the sparks on his feet in Bombay, at least well enough
          for him to fly home, went for a celebration swim in the
          hotel pool, was landed on by an Italian —
PENNY: — a Greek —
FRANK: — doing a bellyflop, only her head was in the way, so
          now she's in hospital with a suspected fractured neck.
          The sparks is back in England, Penny was working on
          an antiques programme —
PENNY: — collectables —
FRANK: — in Bristol, Denis rings her, here she is, only four
          days after we started, everything's terriff. She just got
          in by train.
          [PENNY *smiles weakly.*]
PENNY: Hello, everybody. Isn't it hot?
FRANK: Penny's never been abroad before.
PENNY: It's so hot. Are you Mr Fuller?
MARTIN: Yes.
PENNY: And is this Mrs Fuller?
SALLY: No.
          [MEHTA *appears. He is shy and smiling.*]
MEHTA: Mr Frank, I have been to the station. It is not possible
          to use the railway telegraph for the purpose you require
          without authorisation from Railway Bhavan Delhi.
          And first, for application to write letter to Railway

Bhavan, you must see Regional Director here, Mr Gopalswami on Wednesday, one o'clock.

FRANK: Everybody in the crew bus! Up to the temple!

> [*They all tramp across the stage,* FRANK *herding* MEHTA. *Once there they surround* MEHTA, *touching pulling, advising — the effect is what a casual beggar might observe.* MEHTA *is being readied for his first film break. Quite suddenly* MEHTA *finds the clapper board under his nose; he is clapped silently by* FRANK; *the others melt away. He is alone. He puts on his glasses with the elaboration of an American defence attorney and then begins, in a sing-song voice.*]

MEHTA: 'In the year nine hundred eight five was born Rajaraja, great King, also known as Rajaraja the Great, of the Cola dynasty, who invaded Ceylon and was building in his time many temples but not this one. Why do I mention Rajaraja? From his time all temples look like this temple, which has shrine room, garbhargra (not permitted to film or photograph) hall for worshipper, mandappa; joined by short passage or vestibule, antarala. This is all approached as we shall see by porch — [*He indicates it gravely.*] — ardhamandapa. So. You are asking me when was this temple built please. I am replying, this is very old temple. What was happening in this temple? People was worshipping. What was this worship?' What is happening please?

> [*For* FRANK *walks on and puts his arms round* MEHTA. *He is higher than a kite on the best Nepalese shit. He is smiling and kindly.*]

FRANK: Just terriff.

MEHTA: This is good?

FRANK: Triff, A-one.

MEHTA: Was rehearsal.

FRANK: Was a take. Shooting.

MEHTA: [*doubtful*] You have been shooting?

FRANK: It was fabulous.

MEHTA: There is more. I am not into my stride.
FRANK: I can tell. I want you to meet Penny. Penny!
        [*She comes in.*]
        B.A., this is Penny, the P.A. Penny the P.A., this is
        B.A. Now listen, would you be nice enough to buy
        Penny an ice-cream because we just want to go up the
        hill a bit and get a top shot. But don't worry. The bit
        you did was triff.
        [*He wanders off.* MEHTA *looks after him.*]
PENNY: Is it all right for me to show my legs?
MEHTA: What?
PENNY: My legs.
MEHTA: [*abstracted*] Yes, they are used. Many tourists here.
        He's not going to do more here?
PENNY: Dunno. But don't worry about it. Have you seen the
        monkeys?
MEHTA: Yes, temple monkeys. Would you like an ice-cream?
PENNY: Better not. It's very old, isn't it?
MEHTA: Yes.
PENNY: How old are you?
MEHTA: [*grave*] I am forty. You?
PENNY: Twenty-eight. Martin's nice, isn't he?
MEHTA: Yes. He's very nice.
PENNY: How old is *he*?
MEHTA: I — I don't know.
PENNY: I haven't had a chance to change my money yet. That
        woman there: what does she do?
MEHTA: [*tight*] She is a prostitute.
        [PENNY *considers.*]
PENNY: Isn't it hot today?
MEHTA: This is the dry season.
PENNY: I see. Frank's stoned out of his skull. I suppose it's
        cheap out here.
MEHTA: Well —
PENNY: What you did was terrific. Really.
MEHTA: But I didn't do anything.
PENNY: Oh, but you did.
MEHTA: No. I am qualified guide.

PENNY: It was terrific.
MEHTA: I hadn't started.
PENNY: Yes, but...
                    [MEHTA *gazes at her.*]
MEHTA: What, please?
PENNY: You feel you've been exploited. *Don't* feel exploited.
MEHTA: I am not happy with my performance. [*suddenly, in Hindi*] Go away! If you don't go away I'll call the police!
PENNY: What are you saying?
MEHTA: I am telling that one to go away.
PENNY: The lady who is the prostitute.
MEHTA: Yes.
PENNY: Are there many prostitutes in India?
MEHTA: [*embarrassed*] I am not in a position to say.
PENNY: You mean you're not allowed to.
MEHTA: I have no idea.
PENNY: Don't tell me if you don't want to.
                    [*She looks down and sees her Sony Walkman phones on her chest. She puts them over her ears. Sighs, and switches on: probably 'The Eagles' Greatest Hits.' Something crawls over her foot. She screams and clutches at* MEHTA*'s arm.*]
MEHTA: It is harmless. It was an ant.
PENNY: Pardon?
                    [*She can't hear because of the phones.*]

                    [*Blackout.*]

The cutting room. CHRIS *and* FRANK *are slumped, drinking coffee from a takeaway. There are two packs of takeaway food and a pot of coleslaw.*

CHRIS: You're kidding.
FRANK: I'm not.
CHRIS: Little Penny? My little Penny? I don't believe it.
FRANK: I bet you she did. Or he did. What do you want, shrimp or cheese and pineapple? Here.
CHRIS: Shrimp!

FRANK: Well, have the cheese and pineapple if you like. My
brain's packed it in. What was it you asked me to get?
CHRIS: Chicken curry.
FRANK: Yeah, that was it. Have some coleslaw. She gave him
her Sony Walkman when she left.
CHRIS: *Gave* it to him…
FRANK: Quixotic, eh? A quixotic gesture, John. By, she was
bloody useless.
> [CHRIS *laughs*.]
CHRIS: Now come on, Frankie, you don't know for a fact. Not
for a fact.
FRANK: The crew thought so.
CHRIS: That's just because they couldn't have her.
FRANK: Old Tourims was the Spanish waiter. Except that
she'd never been to Spain either. He must have
thought it was Christmas Day.
CHRIS: You know your trouble, Frankie, You've got a vivid
imagination. And she wasn't useless. Her shot lists are
okay. I bet she's a little cracker.
FRANK: Yeah.
CHRIS: Mountain Joy Rides. Good luck to him. Poor kid.
Penny, I mean.
FRANK: This is dangerous sexist nonsense we're talking now.
[*He reflects*.] I don't feel sorry for her. I envy her, in a
way.
> [*He studies* CHRIS.]
Kate is going to work in Brussels.
CHRIS: She's definitely going?
FRANK: Yeah. And I think that should be that.
CHRIS: [*kindly*] 'S'only Brussels. Isn't it?
FRANK: Well?
CHRIS: What about the kids?
FRANK: Friends. For a bit.
CHRIS: It's not a bit, is it?
FRANK: You mean Brussels? I dunno.
CHRIS: Talk about it.
FRANK: No. [*He examines his bread cake*.] What am I eating, the
shrimp or the pineapple?

CHRIS: What does she say about it?
FRANK: About what?
CHRIS: Splitting up?
FRANK: Nothing. She should *say* something?
CHRIS: It was all going on while you was out there, was it?
FRANK: Do me a favour, you mean what went wrong? Nothing. I went wrong. I didn't go wrong, it was the wrong film. You know my mother remembers him well?
CHRIS: Who?
FRANK: Martin. Wonderful, isn't it? She remembers him very well. She said, oh, I know him, he used to win all the prizes, he's that bloke that used to go to your school. He married that girl with the blonde hair. The actress. That's right, the actress. She had a little kiddie. It was all in *The Express*.
CHRIS: What's this got to do with you and Kate?
FRANK: What? How do I know? It needs editing.
CHRIS: You were jealous of him.
    [FRANK *insists mildly, averting the question.*]
FRANK: It needs editing.
    [*Lights down.*]

On the upper stage SALLY *is slumped a little too casually in her chair.* MARTIN *is waiting on his cue mark, ready to walk into shot. They are both looking from time to time for some clue from the invisible crew. Then* MARTIN *walks in. He affects surprise at seeing her. He affects no surprise at all at the presence of* KEITH, *the sound recordist, who is intertwined with the table legs, hidden from camera, and festooned with nagra and gun mike and wires.*

MARTIN: Hello!
SALLY: Hello!
MARTIN: May I —?
    [*But he has trouble with the chair.*]
I thought the chair — it was going to be — the chair is impossible like this.
FRANK: [*off*] Penny. Go and fix the chair.

> [PENNY *comes on with clipboard and stopwatch. She
> studies the chair.*]

PENNY: Is it bad?

MARTIN: [*to* SALLY] I'm sorry.

PENNY: Is it the legs?

MARTIN: No, it's not the legs. The legs are fine. Just the right number, in fact. But it was going to be — I can't slip in behind the table as I would like.

> [PENNY *studies seriously.*]

PENNY: We could move it back.

MARTIN: Good.

PENNY: [*calls off*] Frank? Is it all right if we move the chair back six or seven inches?

FRANK: [*off*] You can chop the bloody chair for firewood if you like. You can get down on your hands and knees and he can sit on you. You can pile Keith's expense claims — I don't care what you do but can we please —?

> [MEHTA *appears helpfully with a chair of a wholly
> different design.* FRANK *is still speaking off.*]

What are you doing?

MEHTA: This chair is better?

FRANK: Oh, bloody *hell*!

> [*They wait. He storms on. He picks up the chair that has
> caused the problem and bangs it down. He takes the chair
> from* MEHTA, *would like to brain him with it, changes
> his mind and hands it back. He points dramatically.*
> MEHTA *slinks off. Now for* MARTIN:]

Now listen. Forget the chair. The chair is perfect. Go back to your mark. Wait for my cue. Walk in. 'Hello.' 'Hello.' 'May I sit down?' 'Yes, for sure.' 'Oh sod it, look, the chair's too close to the table. I'll just move it shall I?' 'Yes, why not. That's better. Comfy now?' 'Triff. Where were we?' Start the interview. Poise, Martin. Elegance. Swift when the need arises. Decisions. Because I've promised to be home by Christmas. And it's February already.

> [*He pulls the slate from under his arm.*]

[*shouts, spiteful*] Slate 47, take two.

[*He walks out of the shot.* MARTIN *waits on his cue mark. He walks in.*]

MARTIN: Hello.

SALLY: Hi. Why don't you sit down? Move that chair.

MARTIN: Thanks. Pleasant day.

SALLY: Fine.

[*But just as* MARTIN'*s bum hits the seat,* KEITH *speaks from under the table.*]

KEITH: Hold it. This won't work.

FRANK: [*off*] Cut.

[FRANK *walks back in: dangerous.*]

It won't *what?*

KEITH: I'll have to mike them. I can't hear them.

FRANK: Yóu can't *hear* them? You wanted to be under the table.

KEITH: No good, Frank.

FRANK: Triff. You just spent five minutes crawling about under there, arranging yourself. I don't want to mike them. They're meeting by chance.

MARTIN: [*arch, aimed at* SALLY] With just a sound recordist under the table. Just a chance sound recordist.

[FRANK *rounds on him.*]

FRANK: Are you going to wear that thing on the end of your nose for the rest of your life?

MARTIN: I am trying to keep free of infection.

FRANK: There is stuff by-passing that Bandaid right now, this minute, Bank Holiday traffic, *millions* of germs going straight down your gizz — what are half a dozen more on a pimple going to matter?

MARTIN: [*with dignity*] A bite. Not a pimple. A bite.

KEITH: Er, what d'you want me to do, Frank?

FRANK: What's wrong with fishing for it?

KEITH: Shadows. That's the lighting, mate.

FRANK: It's lit this way against all union regulations so I can film the end of Mr Fuller's nose as he would wish. You're saying the only way to get any sound on this is for you to hide under the table —?

SALLY: He's saying that's not the way.

KEITH: I can put a mike on each of them.

FRANK: Then it looks like a —

KEITH: It is. That's what it is. An interview.

FRANK: Where are you going to put the mike on —?

SALLY: [*supplies*] — Sally —

FRANK: Where are you going to put the mike on Sally?

KEITH: [*pats his chest*] Up here.

FRANK: Triff. Dead casual.

MARTIN: How about — just a suggestion — how about miking the flowers?

FRANK: Great. Get the flowers talking to each other, like, and then you and…sort of chip in. A bit *barmy*, Martin. Rodge? Rodge!

> [*But an invisible* RODGE *is sloping off.*]

Where's he going?

KEITH: Want me to mike them?

FRANK: Mike them. What do I care?

KEITH: Be a bit.

FRANK: What do you mean, it'll be a bit?

KEITH: The crew bus is down at the station, getting some Orange Golds.

FRANK: And the radio mikes are in the bus. Great. Okay. Great.

> [*He walks off.*]

KEITH: What's up with him?

MARTIN: You're asking me?

> [KEITH *shrugs and wanders off.* SALLY *is still very calm.* MARTIN *is calm on the outside only. He smiles. He is embarrassed.*]

Shouldn't be long. These things happen. Well.

> [*He gingerly takes a corner of the Bandaid and pulls it off. The pain is excruciating.*]

Arrgh!

SALLY: Painful.

MARTIN: No, I —

SALLY: Your eyes are watering.

MARTIN: Are they? I suppose they are.

SALLY: The man unmasked.

MARTIN: Er, yes.
> [*He stands up and peers this way and that, upstage. His nose is raw.*]

Nice up here. Nice outlook.

SALLY: Good.

MARTIN: The view from the verandah, eh? You seem…

SALLY: …yes?

MARTIN: How are you?

SALLY: It may have slipped your mind, but you were going to come round last night. I think that's what you said. Did you come round?

MARTIN: I knocked at your door.

SALLY: That was you? I opened the door, for God's sake.

MARTIN: I'd, um, run away by then. There was an old man hissing…in the shrubbery.

SALLY: The night-watchman.

MARTIN: I see. And er, in the window — the bedroom —

SALLY: My husband. On a flying visit. He works up at the observatory.

MARTIN: Yes. What's his name — not the night-watchman —

SALLY: Bob. He's gone again now. For a fortnight or so. You were wondering if you got or gave out the wrong signals yesterday.
> [*Pause.*]

MARTIN: Yes.

SALLY: You didn't. Not at all.
> [*He avoids the further possibilities of this, and examines the view again.*]

MARTIN: It *is* beautiful here. Everything you see was imported, you know. Carried up by train, and…everything. Before, there was just jungle. Or scrub, or something. And then…mostly Scotsmen…So it isn't real. I suppose you could say. Artificial. [*He turns.*] But it says something rather wonderful about us all the same. Don't you think? That we can…create…make something lasting and substantial and…that what we've done is *fit*…that's good, isn't it?

SALLY: You mean it shows humankind in a good light.

MARTIN: Yes! Humankind! Oh well, if you like, it's all no more than a huge garden, a garden on a grand scale, but there's enough jungle in the world, God knows…and not half enough — would you accept the place as a metaphor for culture?

SALLY: Unfamiliar territory that. For me.

MARTIN: Culture.

SALLY: Metaphor. Is that what we're going to talk about, on the film?

MARTIN: Christ no. At least…

SALLY: [*patient*] What are we going to talk about?

> [*But before* MARTIN *can probe this unsatisfactory answer,* FRANK *wanders in with slices of melon on a broad leaf. He sets it down on the table and picks up a slice for himself.*]

FRANK: A woman for duty, a boy for pleasure, but a melon for ecstasy. Shakespeare. Henry the Fourth, Part One.

MARTIN: Should you be eating this? [*to* SALLY] Do you eat off the street?

FRANK: It's not off the street. It's from the hotel fridge. It's been washed in distilled water and Dettol, two parts to one and sliced by American-trained surgeons under clinical conditions. It's been passed by Fruit and Vegetable Bhavan, Delhi. Have some.

> [SALLY *shakes her head, but* MARTIN *picks up a bit and eats, gingerly.* FRANK *smiles grimly.*]

Great, eh?

MARTIN: [*complains through a mouthful*] It's not chilled at all.

SALLY: He bought it in the street downstairs. There's a stall behind the hotel.

> [MARTIN *has a mouthful. He can't spit it. He can't swallow it.* FRANK *smiles.*]

FRANK: I see your pimple's decided to brazen it out.

> [MARTIN *swallows.*]

MARTIN: I think I'd just like to freshen up. If you'll excuse me. Shan't be a tick.

> [*He leaves.* FRANK *sits down and eats busily.*]

FRANK: Gone to use his *Sunday Times* Special Offer Stomach

Pump. He told you about himself?

SALLY: Yes. Quite a lot. He also said he wrote books.

FRANK: Children's books. My kids read them. You know 'Marry, my lady, the King of Spain hath shown this crown of England great scorn.' Yeah, well…the books are good. What d'you think of him?

SALLY: Tell me about you.

FRANK: I'm *hot*. This is a hot country. I think my brain is sweating. [*He laughs*.] And the dope is really strong, you know?

SALLY: Do you like it here?

FRANK: India? This town? Here? I could busk it. How about you? What do you do, by the way?

SALLY: Nothing.

FRANK: For bread, I mean?

SALLY: Nothing.

FRANK: You came out here to find yourself.

SALLY: Yes.

FRANK: [*laughs*] And now you have, you're disappointed.

SALLY: No. Now I'm in perfect balance.

[MARTIN *walks back on, in a fresh shirt.*]

MARTIN: Here we are. Ready to go again. Keith back?

FRANK: Sit down a minute, Martin. Let's be sensible. What are you going to say? What's Sally going to say?

MARTIN: [*suddenly defensive*] You mean what's the point?

FRANK: In a nutshell, yes.

[MARTIN *stands up again, agitated.*]

MARTIN: I — You have said that every time I've proposed something. You have said that practically on the hour every day since a week last Tuesday. What was the point of the water-buffalo?

FRANK: Dunno.

MARTIN: And yet you spent over three hours — you spent an entire afternoon — didn't you? —

FRANK: Mmm.

MARTIN: Then what's the point of holding this conversation about the point?

SALLY: [*offers*] I can go.

MARTIN: No. You sit tight. I particularly want you to be in this
          film. [*to* FRANK] Does that answer your question?
SALLY: Why?
MARTIN: What? Never mind that for a moment. This is some-
          thing I have to clear up with Frank. Does that answer
          your question, Frank?
FRANK: You would like…?
SALLY: — Sally —
FRANK: — Sally — to be in the film.
MARTIN: Exactly. That is my wish. As far as I understood my
          brief from your Executive Producer —
FRANK: — Denis —
MARTIN: Yes, Denis — the film was to be seen through my eyes.
          Well. Eh?
                   [*He smirks. But if he expects that to clinch the argu-
                   ment, he doesn't know television.*]
FRANK: [*calm*] Bullshit.
MARTIN: I see.
                   [*A stony silence.*]
          Thank you.
SALLY: Whereabouts did you film the water-buffalo?
MARTIN: [*indignant*] Oh, we had to get off the train to do that.
          We had to hire a goat lorry.
FRANK: [*derisive*] A goat lorry.
MARTIN: Yes! A goat lorry and drive back along the track.
                   [FRANK *turns to* SALLY.]
FRANK: I don't know where it was. I just saw them out of the
          train windows. Triff. Six of them. In an orangey-red
          mud-bath, by the sides of a river.
MARTIN: [*nettled*] Yes, yes —
FRANK: On which were dancing dragonflies. With a sunset
          and a lady in a white sari. And in the background a
          bloke on a bicycle, holding a black sun umbrella.
MARTIN: I was *there*.
FRANK: You were in the goat lorry, sulking.
MARTIN: Doing what?
FRANK: Sulking. You were sulking and reading a book by Roy
          Hattersley.

MARTIN: [*with great dignity*] I was reading a book by Claude Lévi-Strauss.

FRANK: What's the difference?

MARTIN: What's the — exactly!

> [*He is furious.* KEITH *wanders back in. He has a pin microphone which has to be attached to* SALLY*'s bosom. The lead goes down the front of her shirt on the inside. Round her waist, tied by tapes, goes the battery. This is one of the perks of* KEITH*'s job, fixing up radio mikes onto good-looking girls. While the quarrel between* FRANK *and* MARTIN *heightens,* SALLY *submits in patience to having her clothing disarranged from her neck to her crotch.*]

FRANK: All right, you were reading a book by Clause Levi-Strauss. Great. What's the difference? You were reading a book, man.

MARTIN: Now I don't want to start a quarrel — I most definitely do not want to waste time on futile argument at this stage.

> [*Out of the corner of his eye he is aware of the business with* KEITH *and* SALLY.]

I do not want to add to the problems we are all — good God, what is Keith doing?

SALLY: [*calm*] Undressing me.

FRANK: All I asked was what point the interview has. All right? We can do it. Great. Roger could be back by nightfall —

KEITH: [*absorbed*] Gone down to the station.

FRANK: For orangeade. The cameraman's just popped off for a dozen ethnic Tizers from his personal supplier, he'll be back by nightfall almost for sure. Penny's gone to do poo-poos. As soon as Keith has checked out —

SALLY: Sally.

FRANK: — yeah, Sally, and providing the batteries haven't gone down, provided there's some tape in the machine, and as soon as I've rolled myself a bloody great joint the size of a courgette, we can do it. We can start. Triff. I'm agreeing with you. [*He suddenly shouts.*]

But what the fuck are we doing it *for*?
[MEHTA *arrives with briefcase.*]
MEHTA: I am interrupting?
FRANK: [*bellows*] Will you get out of here?
[*Blackout.*]

MARTIN *and* FRANK *are slumped in chairs, having exhausted themselves in argument.*

MARTIN: Well.
FRANK: It's no big deal.
MARTIN: It was very stupid of me to lose my temper.
[FRANK *shrugs. Silence.*]
I think it was pretty irresponsible of me to agree to do this film.
[FRANK *sighs impatiently. Silence.*]
What does that mean?
FRANK: You haven't done the film. You're giving up before you've started. It's a film. That's all it is. It's an hour's worth of pretty pictures. It doesn't say a blind word about what it's like to be Tourims, or his cousin, or the people on the road who live in misery. It isn't that kind of film. It's about you, Martin.
MARTIN: Maybe that's what's making me miserable.
FRANK: Why?
MARTIN: Is that the film *you* would want to make? About the people on the road.
FRANK: How do I know?
MARTIN: Don't you? I mean, don't you have an opinion?
FRANK: What am I, a monster? I have a thousand fucking opinions. But I thought *you* were going to say something. About happiness.
MARTIN: [*absent*] Balance.
FRANK: Balance, then.
MARTIN: It's hardly working out that way, is it?
FRANK: You're the writer. I can't tell you what to say.
MARTIN: You don't think we ought to...I don't know...do it differently...?

FRANK: I don't.

MARTIN: Do I sound as though I'm ashamed of myself?

FRANK: I dunno. Are you? Really?

MARTIN: I think so. Yes.

FRANK: No good. I want to be happy. See?

MARTIN: I am lost, Frank.

FRANK: Bullshit.

MARTIN: Lost.

FRANK: You're not lost. You're lazy. Well, of course you are. You want to busk it, stay at all the piss-elegant hotels, meet the country's leading judges and agricultural experts and all the rest of it, and knock off a little essay. But what for? You looked at a map in England and chose this place to be happy in. This particular place. I have to know why. What makes you happy, what you mean by it, what stops you in your tracks.

MARTIN: The fact is, not to put too fine a point on it, I'm not happy.

FRANK: Then bleeding well get happy. Penny tells me you booked a call to your agent today.

MARTIN: Yes.

FRANK: What happened?

MARTIN: She hadn't come back from lunch.

FRANK: All you've got to do, Martin, is tell me something I didn't already know about you. Or couldn't guess. That's all.

MARTIN: I'm having trouble, Frank.

FRANK: Then fake it. What about this Sally?

MARTIN: What about her?

FRANK: Getting anywhere?

MARTIN: The lady is married.

FRANK: I know, but *are* you? Getting anywhere? You were buzzing around her last night.

MARTIN: I bought her a drink.

FRANK: Why not go and turn down the covers for her?

MARTIN: In the interests of the film.

FRANK: Well, you're not getting much from me.

MARTIN: This is sound advice, is it?

FRANK: Look man, you won all the prizes at school and all that. You and Victor Ludorum were the best two kids in the school. You're the intellectual of this party.

MARTIN: That qualifies me as a lecher, does it?

FRANK: Maybe she plays chess. Maybe you can go through her old theatre programmes. But for Christ's sake let's get somewhere, Martin. You know, let's enjoy something. If it doesn't sound too vulgar.

   [*He rises.*]

   I'm going to eat. You want to eat?

MARTIN: No. What you're suggesting is disgusting. In a liberal sense it's completely...appalling.

FRANK: Really?

MARTIN: It doesn't begin to touch what this film's about.

FRANK: That's what I'm asking you Martin. What *is* this film about? What do you want to happen?

MARTIN: What do I want to *happen*?

   [*A very slow fade to black as* FRANK *leaves, leaving* MARTIN *slumped.*]

A match is struck, illuminating SALLY *in a silk wrap. She has just got out of bed and moved to her living room, where she lights a paraffin lamp.* MARTIN *appears behind her in a cotton bathrobe.* SALLY *glances back.*

SALLY: Did I wake you?

MARTIN: No electric light?

SALLY: There's a power curfew. Your hotel has its own generator. So you wouldn't have noticed.

MARTIN: You look utterly beautiful.

   [*She laughs gently.*]

SALLY: Ah yes. It goes with the night and the stars. It goes with the moon. You look nice. I got up for a pill. [*She smiles.*] A migraine pill.

MARTIN: Oh God, you have migraine?

SALLY: Not if I take the pill. Sit down. This room's cooler than the bedroom. [*Polite. She closes her wrap more securely.*]

Um, have you seen enough for the time being?

MARTIN: I'm sorry. This is…unexpected.

SALLY: It is, isn't it? Bob'll be furious to have missed you. If that doesn't sound too civilised.

MARTIN: Where is he now?

SALLY: I told you, up at the observatory. He's not going to come rushing home, if that's what you mean.

MARTIN: What exactly does he do?

SALLY: I don't know. It's a big place, the observatory. I forget how many million rupees it cost.

MARTIN: How many Europeans are there?

[*She smiles.*]

SALLY: Foreigners, you mean? Twenty. I don't know for certain. About twenty. He loves it. The Indian scientists all read the *New Yorker* and talk about little tratts they found in downtown Denver and all that. There's a lot of glamour.

MARTIN: But you didn't want to live there.

SALLY: No.

[*He rubs his arms under the robe and walks to the imaginary window.*]

MARTIN: I didn't expect to stand on just this spot, looking at stars, when I agreed to do this film. To come out here, I mean. I didn't realise that such a spot existed. This particular spot. I didn't —

SALLY: — don't say it —

MARTIN: I didn't know such as you existed.

SALLY: Well, there we are. [*Pause.*] You're very funny in bed.

MARTIN: Comical.

SALLY: Humorous; and grateful. Don't you have a girl?

MARTIN: No. I am grateful, yes. Are you happy, as you are?

SALLY: You mean with Bob?

MARTIN: I mean what can I do, to see you again? To see you. To continue to see you.

SALLY: Not a right lot, as my father would say. Can you?

MARTIN: Are you? Happy?

SALLY: Oh, Martin…

MARTIN: Because if you weren't happy…assuming that you would like to do something to change it…then…if you were prepared to…

SALLY: Doesn't long distance come into it?

MARTIN: That's something we could overcome.

SALLY: No. I meant, doesn't the fact that you're a long way from home, and working with what seem to me like idiots — doesn't all that affect what you're trying to tell me? I like you. And if you're grateful in bed, you're also generous. Very.

[*She kisses him and then moves away.*]

MARTIN: Flying out here, I happened to glance down out of the window. I don't even know what country it was; it was night, and there were snowy mountains. They were lit by the moon. In the shadow of these mountains, there was a little blob of yellow light, a town. Leading away from it, in a straight line, the sodium lamps, I suppose, of a road. And then blackness. It filled me with dread. To be suspended thirty odd thousand feet above an anonymous town, filled with unknowable people, asleep…and never to know them…And then I met you.

SALLY: I would like you to come back to bed and make love to me.

[*He doesn't move.*]

What's the matter? Isn't that a good idea?

MARTIN: I would like more.

SALLY: Be content.

MARTIN: I would like more.

[*She hesitates.*]

SALLY: [*going*] Put out the lamp, won't you?

[*She leaves.* MARTIN *turns down the wick of the lamp and blows across the glass flue.*]

[*Blackout.*]

END OF ACT ONE

ACT TWO

Spotlit, MEHTA *is standing on the upper stage, singing a plain-tive Indian love song, keening and full of yearning. His light is suddenly extinguished.*

We find on the lower stage, in the cutting room, PENNY. *She is sitting in* CHRIS*'s chair, a huge bazaar bag by her side. She drops her head into her hands and sobs; at which* MARTIN *comes in, wearing a dark suit. He is expecting a crowd.*

MARTIN: Sorry I'm so late, I — Penny! How lovely! What a nice surprise. How are you? What's happened?

PENNY: Nothing.

MARTIN: You're crying.

PENNY: No I'm not.

MARTIN: Course you're not. Bit of a head cold, is it? How are you? May we kiss?
[*She averts her face.*]
How are you?

PENNY: Bloody.

MARTIN: [*uneasy*] Mmm. I mean, really? You look…Have you had your hair cut?

PENNY: No.

MARTIN: You look…Well, I was going to say you look completely different, but then I suppose we all do.

PENNY: You're looking forward to this, are you?

MARTIN: I haven't seen a foot of it. Frank not here?

PENNY: Still at the pub.

MARTIN: Still — it's all-day drinking in Acton is it? Thursday hours?

PENNY: It's only just gone three.
[MARTIN *glances at a digital watch.*]

MARTIN: Three twenty one, actually. And thirty seven seconds.

PENNY: And it's Wednesday, not Thursday. Does it play a tune?

MARTIN: [*startled*] Does it?

PENNY: My nephew has one. You must know what day it is.

MARTIN: Yes. But not with any help from this thing. Is it Thursday in Japan, perhaps? You can change the day of the week but then you lose the time of the day. Of course, I suppose with the computer...Why were you crying? Don't. Not worth it. How's your...um...mother?

PENNY: Back in hospital. How's your book?

MARTIN: Book?

PENNY: That you were going to write.

MARTIN: Likewise. Poorly. I've been — things have been unsettled. Since we got back.

PENNY: No kidding.

MARTIN: Look, I said I would ring you for a drink sometime and in fact I did. But they said you were on leave, or something.

PENNY: [*a hollow laugh*] On leave?

MARTIN: That's what they said.

PENNY: You may as well know I'm chucking all this up and going back. I can't stand it here anymore.

MARTIN: No. You're probably right.

PENNY: I'm sick to death with materialism.

MARTIN: You may have a point. Do you hear from B.A.? Old Tourims?

PENNY: It's got nothing to do with him.

MARTIN: No, of course not. Though he was a very nice man.

PENNY: He was worse than any of you.

MARTIN: Was he?

PENNY: Going to that bloody place opened my eyes.

MARTIN: But I thought you said you were going back.

PENNY: Not to that hellhole.

MARTIN: [*decides*] You feel bitter about it.

PENNY: You don't?

MARTIN: Bitter? I don't know. I feel utterly changed. I don't know why I feel that, and if you talk to anyone about it their eyes start to glaze over. The only ones who want to talk about it are the ones who've been. I didn't realise what a grisly club I'd joined.

PENNY: In other words, it's left you discontented.

MARTIN: Yes.

PENNY: I'm leaving today. I came here to give Frank his expense claims. Yours are there as well. I don't want any more to do with it. Television, I mean. Frank. You. Anything. I'm walking out as soon as they get back.

MARTIN: Can you do that?

PENNY: Try and stop me.

MARTIN: Have you seen any of it? The film. I mean?

PENNY: It's the same old lies. You look terrible on it. What a rotten country this is.

MARTIN: Isn't it. [*Pause.*] Well, no it isn't actually.

    [PENNY *suddenly puts her head in her hands and sobs.*]

PENNY: I hate everybody.

MARTIN: Oh, here, here…Penny, love…

PENNY: I'm so unhappy.

MARTIN: Of course you're not.

PENNY: I am! I know whether I'm unhappy or not!

MARTIN: Of course you do. It's old B.A., is it? Old Tourims? He hasn't let you down, has he? I bet he has. What a rotter. The swine.

PENNY: I love him!

MARTIN: Of course you do. Here. Come and have a cuddle. Have a good cry. Let it all out.

PENNY: He just wouldn't believe it was happening. He wouldn't believe I was a serious person. I *am* a serious person. He wouldn't listen, never listened, just went on waggling his head —

    [*Unconsciously* MARTIN *is waggling his head in imitation of* MEHTA.]

— and went on and on at what a lovely girl I was, as if he'd never seen a naked woman before in his life.

MARTIN: Well —

PENNY: And you! You all thought it was so comical. Oh yes, you as well. 'Little Penny'…Calling him Tourims. Trying to get us into bed, well, we didn't need you. Let me go.

    [*She breaks free of him and starts to root about in her carry bag for tissues. There is an awful lot of* PENNY *in that bag.*]

MARTIN: Here. Take my hanky.
PENNY: I have some tissues here, thank you very much. Here's foulmouth's expenses, and here's yours. I'm not waiting for them to come back from the pub. And don't touch that machine, unless you want the whole building to be blacked. I didn't ask to go, remember. It was never intended that I should go, in the first place. And I found what I was looking for, except that when I found it I didn't know what I was looking for. And you can laugh as much as you like.
MARTIN: I'm a very long way from laughing.
PENNY: There's a coffee machine down the hall. You need twos and ones to make it work.
> [MARTIN *picks up the papers she has scattered on the Steenbeck and puts them straight. Then he exclaims and punches the Steenbeck button bad-temperedly.*]
MARTIN: Shit!

'India'. SALLY *is alone and* MARTIN *is asking her questions out of vision. She is gay, and amused. But she is also quite nervous of the camera. All* MARTIN'*s lines are delivered from the lower stage.* SALLY *is at first waiting for her cue.*

MARTIN: How long have you lived here?
SALLY: Three years. I —
MARTIN: No, go on —
SALLY: I was going to ask you why you came here to film.
MARTIN: Because…I'd been told it was very beautiful.
SALLY: You think so?
MARTIN: Yes, of course. Do you?
SALLY: [*thoughtful*] Yes…I suppose so. It's very quiet.
> [*She laughs at the lack of a follow-up question.*]
MARTIN: Are you happy here?
SALLY: I never ask myself. Nobody ever asks me. I have a husband — do you want to hear about my husband?
MARTIN: Not really, but go on; start again with 'I have a husband.'
SALLY: I have a husband who works up at the observatory, up

there. It's a tracking station as well, that sort of thing. It's very modern, they're proud of it. [*Pause.*] Is this really worth saying?

MARTIN: It's agreeable here — the climate, the scenery, and so on. Do you ever feel cut off from the real world?

SALLY: I've felt cut off from the real world ever since I started to think. [*Pause.*] Which isn't much good to you either.

FRANK: [*off*] Keep running.

[SALLY *laughs again.*]

SALLY: What do you mean, keep running? I don't feel cut off from the real world just because the place is agreeable. I'd have to know what you meant by that. I quite like being on my own.

FRANK: [*off*] What sort of things do you do?

SALLY: Who's asking the questions?

FRANK: [*off*] What sort of things do you do?

SALLY: I go for long walks at night. There are lakes here — well, reservoirs anyway — and I sometimes go and sit by them. I look at my reflection in the water. I go nude bathing with the little boys up there. [*She laughs, hesitates, and then:*] It's very real. I collect pebbles. I make my own clothes. I avoid questions.

FRANK: [*off*] You're a smart-arse, in fact.

SALLY: [*smiling*] All the time, Frank.

[*Sudden blackout.*]

CHRIS *and* FRANK *have come back from the pub.* MARTIN *is looking guilty.* CHRIS *is putting the picture back in sync.*

MARTIN: I'm sorry.

FRANK: Naughty boy.

MARTIN: Perhaps I was tired of waiting. Do you know what time it is, either of you? It's — it's about half past three.

FRANK: Been looking at old smart-arse.

MARTIN: I thought the film was cut.

FRANK: It is.

CHRIS: You can't use that, though.

FRANK: Why not?

CHRIS: You can't. How are you, Martin?

MARTIN: Extremely angry.

FRANK: No you're not. What was the matter with Penny?

MARTIN: I leave you to find out. You've got a bloody cheek, Frank.

FRANK: Sit down. Relax. We've got a fabulous little movie. Forget that bit, it was just an idea. There's some lovely stuff. Isn't there, Chris?

CHRIS: Lovely.

FRANK: That's right, there is. Now listen. This afternoon, you write the script. Right? A few little wordies.

MARTIN: Write the script?

FRANK: The links. Of course write the script. No problems.

MARTIN: A few wordies.

FRANK: That's it.

MARTIN: Now you listen to me —

FRANK: Haven't got time. Did I write you earlier, asking if you wanted to come in and see some of it? Have I rung you up like three hundred times?

MARTIN: You rang me once at three o'clock in the morning.

CHRIS: We've got to know where the narration's going, see, Martin.

MARTIN: It is absolutely out of the question for me to write the script in one afternoon.

FRANK: Let me explain something. Tomorrow morning, Chris is going to have to break all this down into tracks. The next time you see it whole — the next time any of us do — will be at the dub. So we have to have some commentary, like now, like yesterday, as a guide.

MARTIN: I haven't seen a foot of the film.

FRANK: That's right, you haven't.

MARTIN: No. No, definitely no. It's impossible. I mean we go to all the trouble of *going* there —

FRANK: All in the past. All gone. What's over there isn't, any longer. It's here. Two reels.

MARTIN: I'd like to talk to Denis.

FRANK: Denis has got the sack.

MARTIN: When?

FRANK: Tuesday.
MARTIN: Denis has gone?
FRANK: Show business.
MARTIN: Well, who's in charge?
FRANK: I am. If you like. Nobody's ever in charge of anything,
           Martin. But I am.
MARTIN: Denis has *gone*?
FRANK: Any pity would be misplaced. He's gone to breakfast
           television. Look, you've got money in this. I've got
           money in it. Chris starts cutting something else in a
           fortnight. It's show business.
MARTIN: [*agitated*] I happen to have invested a certain amount
           of…*something*…in this film, and —
FRANK: Good. What?
MARTIN: What?
FRANK: That's why we need the wordies.
MARTIN: You mean you genuinely think we can cobble together
           — is that the inhouse word for it — cobble together a
           script in an afternoon and then just go off and have
           dinner and bye-bye India.
FRANK: That's the plan.
MARTIN: What if I say no?
FRANK: Then we're in ze soup.
MARTIN: Chris?
CHRIS: Nothing to do with me.
MARTIN: Stretch yourself. Have an opinion.
CHRIS: In my opinion, you're wasting time.
           [MARTIN *considers, glances at his watch which he has
           taken off his wrist in agitation. He hurls it from him in
           despair.*]
MARTIN: Fuck!

MEHTA *is alone on the upper stage. He is declaiming gently and
hypnotically in his sing-song voice.*

MEHTA: 'What can we make of these melancholy bygones,
           these moments that flee from our understanding like
           snowballs in front of the cooking fire? Where is coming

from? Where is going to? The life of man is short. These questions he carries with him through painful journey from eternity to eternity. He is not getting pleasure from material existence. He is asking questions of his wealth or poverty and nothing is coming back. Please. On this magic mountain, sacred to Hindu, we see the earth touch with the sky, and the one commune with the other, mother talking to father...the under-world which is darkness and unconscious, and the overworld which is demonstrating light of reason. And here, what is not height only, but centre, or joining, British are building what is called hill station. Why are doing this? Because they wish to be cool in summer, and be most like at home in old country. But this, I am already telling you and now I am emphasising also, is sacred mountain, with power to explain, in symbol and myth, meaning of life and why we are here. Which is to say why we are here, not here, but here on earth.'

FRANK: [*off*] And cut!

      [FRANK *walks on, smoking a joint, amused.*]

      Terrifo.

MEHTA: You are sure?

FRANK: Certain. It's great, man.

MEHTA: These words are sufficient?

FRANK: These words are blinding. This, the opening of the film. Perfect. Now we get the sunset.

MEHTA: Sunset?

FRANK: The sun going down. Sunset.

MEHTA: You have not enough sunsets?

FRANK: A film like this, John, you can't have enough sunsets.

MEHTA: But —

FRANK: No buts. Just ace. Clear as crystal.

MEHTA: You see, Mr Frank, this is Jung.

FRANK: Triff. It's what?

MEHTA: Carl Gustav —

FRANK: — don't tell me.

MEHTA: This I must tell you.

FRANK: No, don't tell me. Tell Martin. Martin!
[MARTIN *enters, elated. He shakes* MEHTA *by the hand, his other hand on the Indian's forearm.*]

MARTIN: B.A., that was — I can't tell you how much that was — wasn't it wonderful, Frank?

FRANK: Wonderful. Listen, I've got to go and shoot the sunset. You two sit here and chat.

MEHTA: Chinwag.

FRANK: [*going*] Exactly.

MARTIN: Wonderful. Truly.

MEHTA: I have noticed, in this way of shooting, what you think is never finished. There is always sunset. What is happening in England, people cannot see sunset?

MARTIN: I know what you mean.

MEHTA: Last night, you were going to come to my house.

MARTIN: I — I'm sorry. I…went to see…Sally.

MEHTA: Well, I have prepared special sweetmeats. My sister is making them.

MARTIN: Yes, I am truly sorry. It was unforgiveable of me to forget. Frank was also invited, was he?

MEHTA: Oh yes, he came.

MARTIN: He did.

MEHTA: He was very drunk. You will tell me please, what place in the scheme of things has the principle of yearning?

MARTIN: Yearning? Oh, *yearning*. Is it principled? I thought it just sort of hit you sideways from time to time.

MEHTA: No, this is not yearning.
[MARTIN *looks at him kindly.*]
You wish to say?

MARTIN: I was going to say we must seem a rum lot. But I would like you to believe that I do, genuinely, envy you.

MEHTA: You live in London, I think.

MARTIN: Yes. Is that what you yearn to do?

MEHTA: Of course.

MARTIN: Do you have a picture of what you would be, if you lived in London?

MEHTA: Oh yes. I would be different person.

MARTIN: Is that ever possible?

MEHTA: When you are poor, Martin, it is necessary to think this. You do not like my country.

MARTIN: That isn't — can't be — the case. I don't know it.

MEHTA: Penny doesn't know it. But she likes it.

MARTIN: Penny…?

MEHTA: Yes. She cannot express her thoughts, but she does. She is not afraid.

[MARTIN *searches the landscape*.]

MARTIN: It is beautiful at this time of night. I don't know what I was looking for, but I haven't found it. Perhaps it wasn't very well thought out in the first place. Hot countries have their own special lure, you know. Abandonment perhaps: perhaps that was what I was seeking. Of a fairly discreditable kind. The sun, of course. And brown bodies…you see a girl's long back stooping over a bundle, or huge eyes glancing at you… it must offend you, that kind of yearning.

MEHTA: Such thoughts are unworthy.

MARTIN: Most yearning is.

MEHTA: On this I must beg to differ.

MARTIN: How much more proof do you want, of what we're like? You think you'll be content in London: I thought I could say something out here. Frank's the realistic one. He starts frustrated and angry, he comes out slugging. His head's an ashtray, he has as much sensitivity as a ship's anchor, but he knows something we don't.

MEHTA: Frank is not a deep man.

MARTIN: No, he isn't.

MEHTA: Then you can't help?

MARTIN: Help?

MEHTA: If one was wishing to come to London?

MARTIN: B.A., truly, how on earth can I help?

MEHTA: You are an important man. You are a man of influence.

MARTIN: I am utterly without influence.

MEHTA: You have many shirts, many suits. You are writer.

MARTIN: [*sad*] You can't possibly know how sad this is making me. I have no influence. I don't — I write for children.

I couldn't begin to describe where I am, who I am…in London…If you decide to come, I'll do everything in my power to help — that goes without saying. But it won't be very much.

MEHTA: Penny told me this is what you would say.

MARTIN: Penny again.

MEHTA: Yes. She is my friend.

MARTIN: [*hesitates*] Of course. Did you know that Frank and I went to the same school? Years apart, of course, but we went to the same school, and were taught by some of the same people. What I got out of it was the absolute necessity of saying, as my first position on anything: I don't know. Do you understand what I'm saying? Between him and me there is a divide. What I am now, what I do, the person I am, is wholly made up of doubt and uncertainty. In which, God help me, I take a kind of pride. You want to come to England: I will stop myself from saying this would be a disastrous move. I will say instead I just don't know. Keith!

KEITH: It's pitch bleeding dark up here. Who's that with you?

MARTIN: B.A.

KEITH: Oh yeah. Now listen, Tourims, where's my sari you were going to get me?

MEHTA: You don't wish to choose?

KEITH: How would I know what to choose?

MEHTA: It is for wife?

KEITH: For mother. You nit.

MEHTA: Your mother is old lady?

KEITH: She's forty six, mate. Take Penny with you. She'll know.

MEHTA: Where is Penny, please?

KEITH: Dunno. Up there somewhere.

MEHTA: She is alone?

KEITH: I dunno.

MARTIN: What have you been recording?

KEITH: Wildtrack. Gnats piss. The soft hiss of gnats and the croaking of bleeding glow-worms. With the occasional tweet, crackle of twigs, and mouse fart. According to

Cecil B. De Mille up there there should be a flute playing down in the valley.

MEHTA: No, he is not playing.

KEITH: A mate of yours.

MEHTA: When he is playing, he is playing for money. I have told Frank this one will play good music, but first, there must be money.

KEITH: According to Frank, he plays every night at sunset for the hell of it.

MEHTA: For the hell of it?

MARTIN: Because he likes to.

MEHTA: He doesn't like to. He is playing only because television crews are paying him to play. When is not being paid, he is working in shoe shop. Please, Keith, where is Penny?

KEITH: Never mind about that. I want my sari. If *I* go, I'll be rooked rotten, so I want you to go and say it's for *your* mother. Only explain it has to be sewn up the sides to make a dress, somehow. I've been in there. Fella started talking to me in Italian. Do I *look* Italian?

MEHTA: [*distressed*] Martin. I must tell you one thing. Here there are steep cliffs where in olden days sacrifice was flung over —

MARTIN: Penny!

KEITH: ⎫
           ⎬ Penny!
MARTIN: ⎭

MARTIN: You should have kept an eye on her.

KEITH: I was working. She should have gone with Frank.

MARTIN: Why didn't she?

> [*A roll of thunder.*]

KEITH: Bloody marvellous.

ALL: Penn-ee!

> [*They wander off in all directions as the stage grows dark. Another roll of thunder.*]

For a second or so it is dark. Then the terrible hiss of tropical rain and PENNY *is illuminated in a crackle of lightning. She is soaking wet and her blouse has been torn apart. Her skirt has gone. She is covered in red mud.*

PENNY: Help! Help me someone, please!
    [MEHTA *arrives, also drenched.*]
MEHTA: What is it, what is it?
PENNY: Children!
MEHTA: You are cut, you are wounded?
PENNY: Children! They scratched me. They *scratched* me.
MEHTA: This is not possible.
PENNY: Don't tell me it's not possible, you bastard. It happened. Where are you going? Don't leave me.
    [*But he has gone only a few paces to retrieve her skirt.*]
MEHTA: Here.
    [MARTIN *and* KEITH *call for her, off.*]
The others.
PENNY: [*sharp*] Don't call them. They tried to push me over.
MEHTA: There is some blood on your leg. This hanky, please.
PENNY: In the dark. They tried to push me over.
MEHTA: No, this hasn't happened.
PENNY: Will you stop saying that? What's the matter with you? Why won't you look at me? *Look* at me.
MEHTA: Please. Put on your skirt. Do as I say.
    [*She cries out and runs into his arms.*]

    [*Blackout.*]

The hotel. KEITH *and* MARTIN *are slumped in chairs, quite drunk.* KEITH *is listening to his expensive 5-band radio, with neat little earphones. He quotes from the World Service.*

KEITH: '...Hampshire two hundred and thirty four for eight. No play in the match between Somerset and Glamorgan, because of rain.'
MARTIN: Good.
KEITH: What?
MARTIN: I said: good. The heavens have parted, Keith. Jupiter

Pluvius has hurried down to Taunton with his watering can.
KEITH: Wha'?
MARTIN: Never mind. I said: never mind.
KEITH: Think she's fallen over the precipice?
MARTIN: Very likely.
KEITH: Bloody useless, he is.
MARTIN: Frank.
KEITH: No, Tourims. I asked him two days ago to get me a sari from the sari shop. Shouldn't be difficult.
MARTIN: If she has fallen over a precipice, it will be because Frank's native cruelty, which passes itself off as a sense of humour, left the poor kid there while he went to film an all-important sunset.
KEITH: You think Frank's cruel, do you?
MARTIN: [*bursts out*] Have you any idea of what I might have said about this place, given the chance? I mean I do happen to have read it all up.
KEITH: History, you mean?
MARTIN: Yes, Keith. History.
KEITH: That's not what Frank's after.
MARTIN: I am by now fairly expert on what Frank's against. But what's he for?
KEITH: [*holds up a finger*] Frank.
MARTIN: Right.
KEITH: Numero uno. It's always the same on these hot country jobs. It was the same in Sumatra. Same in Ecuador. Just the same in Taiwan. [*He reflects.*] Singapore was better. But it was the same in Cairo. Khartoum…well. Bulgaria…it was the same there — no! It was worse in Bulgaria. You travel a lot in your job, when you're not drinking?
MARTIN: I know Europe quite well. France, Germany. Italy. Portugal. A little.
KEITH: The same?
MARTIN: Yes. What are we talking about?
KEITH: You know Willesden Green?
MARTIN: Yes…

KEITH: The Bricklayers?

MARTIN: Um…

KEITH: That's my place, mate.

MARTIN: Your pub.

KEITH: My place. My — whatever was you were spouting today — 'my journey towards the unknowably familiar.'

MARTIN: Yes, I remember you giving me some advice on the phrase.

KEITH: You can't help it, can you? That's education. The great stumbling block. You take this contentment, right? When I was at school, I wanted to be an airline pilot. I thought it was a class idea. My father had this job, he used to run stuff up to Heathrow in a van. He falls in with this stewardess. Lynn, they called her. Anyway, he had quite a big thing with her in the death. She lived right out the other side at Theydon Bois; but on the North Circular and that, he could bomb round there in no time.

MARTIN: We're on the track of something here are we, Keith?

KEITH: He used to take her to some ritzy places. Like he used to take her drinking in Orange Street, behind the National Gallery.

MARTIN: Not the Bricklayers.

KEITH: He couldn't go there. He was on the darts team.

MARTIN: And to cut a long story short, it turned out Lynn played for British Airways.

KEITH: Nothing so simple. She was a water-skier. Welsh Harp.

MARTIN: But contentment does come into this, does it?

KEITH: He was banging the arse off this Lynn and coming on strong he had his own road haulage business, and I think he even went so far as to go to the theatre with her. He took swimming lessons. As I say, it was a big thing. One night, he introduced me to her. This is my boy Keith, he said. He wants to be an airline pilot. And she said to me Keith she said, an airline pilot is just a bus driver with headphones on.

MARTIN: I see. Well, you make your point.

KEITH: I haven't finished. See, that's your problem, you don't listen. You're making patterns all the time. I walk home, and there's my Auntie Carole, my mother's sister, in the kitchen. Yes, she says, you've been with your father and that water-ski-ing tart. Well, you can tell him from me I'm going to cut his balls out with this breadknife. And she showed me this breadknife.
         [*Pause.*]
MARTIN: Where was your mother?
KEITH: Earholing. She was ironing, actually.
MARTIN: And?
KEITH: I thought it was interesting.
MARTIN: It is. Fascinating.
KEITH: It isn't now. It was then.
MARTIN: You'll despise me for asking this, Keith, but what happened?
KEITH: She married an airline pilot.
MARTIN: Lynn.
KEITH: Well of course, Lynn, who else?
MARTIN: That's it, is it? Your statement on contentment?
KEITH: You have these dreams when you're a kid. You have these what I think you called yesterday 'figmentary visions'. Or dreams. I don't suppose you started out in life wanting to be a writer, for instance. We all end up as someone else. I don't know whether you know this, but all the cells in the body are replaced — all of them — every seven years. So if you live to be…say…sixty three…you've already been nine people. I did a *Horizon* on it once, in New York. It's the same there. How do you think it's going, the film?
MARTIN: The same.
KEITH: The same? Oh yeah. How do you mean?
MARTIN: The same as you've just been saying.
KEITH: Oh. Yeah. [*Long pause.*] Right.

MEHTA *is sitting on a chair in his shirt and slacks, but without his socks and shoes.* PENNY *is in her full-length nightie. She moves to him and kisses his hair. He is looking shell-shocked.*

PENNY: You didn't have to get dressed.

MEHTA: I *wished.*

PENNY: What's the matter.

> [MEHTA *jerks himself out of his agony.*]

MEHTA: Your scratches. They are better?

> [PENNY *plucks up the hem of her nightie to look. He looks away.*]

PENNY: You don't believe me, do you — that it was children? It was children, dirty little beggar children. Why couldn't it be? Don't dress. Stay with me.

MEHTA: This I can't do.

PENNY: Why not?

MEHTA: The wedding. I must see the father of the bride. There is much to arrange.

PENNY: Is it here?

MEHTA: No, he wants a village wedding.

PENNY: Is it someone you know?

MEHTA: [*nettled*] Why do you say this? You think everybody is known to me, you think we are all from one mother, one father?

PENNY: What's the matter?

MEHTA: Nothing.

PENNY: Good. Talk about something else.

MEHTA: In what English city do you live?

PENNY: Just now? In Bristol. I have a flat in London.

MEHTA: Where, please?

PENNY: Fulham. You know where that is? [*Stony silence.*] I share it with an actress.

MEHTA: Film actress?

PENNY: No. Didn't you want to go to bed with me?

MEHTA: I must leave.

PENNY: You can't. I've hidden your socks and shoes.

MEHTA: They will discover our transaction.

PENNY: Not from me they won't.

MEHTA: The hotel, I mean.

PENNY: Oh, fuck the hotel.

MEHTA: [*winces*] Please...

PENNY: Listen, listen to me please. I am happy now. Do you understand?

MEHTA: [*anguished*] How, happy?

PENNY: *Happy*. Relaxed. Content. Do you think I do this sort of thing all the time? Evidently you do.

MEHTA: Also, this is not my way.

PENNY: Not a film actress, no. You have a funny idea of foreigners. What do you think it's like in London, in Fulham? Not very ritzy. The girl I share with is only an actress because she says she's an actress. She's a creep. She's full of shit. The whole place is. It's hell. Lies, deception, abuse.

MEHTA: What do you think it's like here?

PENNY: *Nothing* like London. Look, you came back for a shower, that was all, and the rest happened. If you want to feel virtuous, it happened because I made it happen. But please. I'm begging you to stay. We'll order a meal, have it sent up.

MEHTA: I can't.

PENNY: You can. Don't be ashamed of me.

MEHTA: I am ashamed of myself.

PENNY: Are you going to try and tell me this hasn't happened to you before, is that what you're trying to get me to believe?

MEHTA: It has happened before.

PENNY: Often.

MEHTA: [*with rage*] Am I telling you often? Yes, it has happened but with party mood and older woman. And not in work situation. And after some acquaintance.

PENNY: On the last night of the tour, in fact.

MEHTA: And without theft of socks and shoes. You, Martin, all of you say you live lies, and are not to be trusted with the truth. But of me you ask for truth; tell me please your women, when, how. You see me just as man. Well, I am not man. I am Indian. I am head of my family.

PENNY: You're married?

MEHTA: [*completely outraged*] You think I am crazy? What do you think I am? You think I am Bombay film-star? I have two brother, three sister. I am BA Tourism Madras, author of pamphlets, associate director of

travel company, qualified tour guide. You think I am
pimp cab-driver? What is wrong with you people?

PENNY: Listen to me. I live by the week in a boarding house in
Bristol. At the weekends I go home to Fulham. I work
in a communications industry, and nobody is ever —
ever — going to ask me what I think, or say now it's
your turn to be creative. There's this great and wonderful industry of people like Frank and Keith and leeches
like Fuller...and I have no-one I can talk to, who's
part of it, unless I want to talk money: or bed. You're
not listening.

MEHTA: I am listening.

PENNY: But not to me.

MEHTA: To the rain. When I leave here — when you give me
back my shoes, I will walk to my house. My sister is
waiting. She will know where all the weddings are to
be, because she is buying rings and bangles from the
market villagers. When she is telling me, I will take
bicycle and go to that place and say: tomorrow there
will come British crew for shooting. Go home then and
wash clothes and talk to my brothers. Make accounts,
then sleep. Money, and sleep.

PENNY: Life isn't money. Money isn't everything.

MEHTA: You are very beautiful. And very rich. Martin is kind.
He is also very rich. You are rich people. This woman
we have seen today, the old woman with the stone
wrapped in rags, striking the rock. You ask me is she
making this rock square, for purposes of building. No.
She is making ballast for the railway. When the rock is
chipped away to nothing, some men bring her another
one. She starts again, little by little, making gravel.
When you come to my house, you can hear her, chop
chop, chop chop. Now Penny, please: give me my
shoes.

> [*Sullenly,* PENNY *reaches down, takes his shoes, and
> tosses them down in front of him.*]

> [*Blackout.*]

MARTIN *stands in the bright light of day.*

MARTIN: 'Weather glorious, earth steaming fiercely from unseasonable cloudburst last night…ants pausing for a moment to gossip about worlds-end flood…'
[*He looks up and grimaces gently.*]
Yes, okay.
[FRANK *walks in and claps the take.*]

FRANK: One oh seven one. One.
[MARTIN *composes himself. But he is getting better at facing the camera.*]

MARTIN: 'Last night, for most of the night, there was rain…the kind of rain that blanks out everything else, throws a curtain in front of your eyes and drowns ants, cobras in their nests, and…by this morning's report…people. Some people who live by the railway, whose official designation is Children of God, but whose existence is somehow strictly unofficial, were swept away, along with a two hundred metre section of track. They had no choice, neither in the matter of where they lived, nor how they came to die. Their huts and shelters, their pieces of cardboard and their torn sacking were all in a cutting, which acted as a gigantic culvert, and they were hit by a flash flood. So far, seven have been recovered. [*Keep running.*] To be here more than a day or so is to realise by how much a European mind is absorbed — is *comforted* by choice. We say: shall I do this today, or shall I do that? Shall I call myself happy…or let myself sink? We say — we all say: maybe I should leave her, or, I ought to chuck this job up and get a croft in Scotland…Or, I think I'd like to work in Australia for a while…When we're on holiday, we say: "Now here's somewhere I could *really* live…" '
[FRANK *walks on unexpectedly. He offers* MARTIN *a few segments of orange, which he refuses.* FRANK *is for once unaggressive.*]
I take it we've stopped.

FRANK: Just changing mags. You okay?

MARTIN: [*dour*] Tickety-boo. Get your film?
  FRANK: Yeah. Have you been down there?
MARTIN: No.
  FRANK: What are we saying, you don't want to do it?
MARTIN: Have they found any more bodies?
  FRANK: Yeah.
MARTIN: You said in London you'd have to show the print of the film to the India High Commission.
  FRANK: Oh for fuck's sake, Martin.
              [KEITH *wanders on.*]
  KEITH: You want to go again?
  FRANK: [*to* MARTIN] What do you want to do?
MARTIN: Okay.
  FRANK: Okay then. Gimme the board, Keith. Turn over. Start running. New slate, one oh eight, one.
              [FRANK *and* KEITH *leave.*]
MARTIN: [*after a sigh*] 'It's part of our thought process to contemplate — no, to luxuriate in change. We say what do you want to happen, or what's going to happen now? The assumption is that chance is like a tap, which we can turn off in the night, having risen to remember that we left it on. Some people have died, of drowning. But out there, or better still down there, on the plain, the temperature is in the hundreds. There, some other people would give their eye teeth for so much as a cup of water. People you and I will never meet, who will never see this film, who could not imagine for what purpose it was being made, even, are living, working, giving birth, burning their dead, watching the sick go grey and turn their face to the wall. This whole place — the hill station, the Garden of Eden — is a preference, a stoutly declared alternative. The rain that washed away the railway squatters has refreshed its every leaf. It was designed by minds like yours and mine to express a preference: better to be us than them. Yesterday, I met a small boy. We crouched on the ground together, and I drew a map of India in the dust. And I found him a pebble, like this

one, and I asked him to place it where he thought he
might live, where he was. He held the pebble in his
hand a long time, looking not at the map, but into my
eyes. I asking the question, do you know where you
are? He with the much better question: what sort of a
question is that? You won't use it, but that's what I
feel.'

> [MARTIN *turns his back on the camera for a moment.
> Then he turns round again.*]

Martin's piece to camera, as requested by his director
over breakfast.

> [FRANK *walks on with two bottles of Orange Gold.*]

FRANK: Here.
MARTIN: I can't drink that stuff.
FRANK: Course you can. It's good.
MARTIN: What is?
FRANK: You getting pissed off.
MARTIN: Good?
FRANK: If that's what you feel.
MARTIN: I feel confused.
FRANK: Isn't that good?
MARTIN: You mean necessary.
FRANK: The Garden of Eden line: triff.
MARTIN: We were flung out of it because we are restless and
ungrateful bastards, Frank.
FRANK: Sally's here.
MARTIN: [*alarmed*] Sally? We agreed she wouldn't come today.
FRANK: I want you to talk to her again. On camera. The two of
you. What we've got of her is just naffo, man. Talk. I
mean, be together.
MARTIN: I don't think so.
FRANK: I need it.
MARTIN: No.
FRANK: She says okay.
MARTIN: She isn't making the film.
FRANK: Neither are you. Hi!

> [SALLY *walks on, calm.*]

SALLY: Hello.

MARTIN: I thought you said — that we agreed —
SALLY: Boredom.
FRANK: Keep talking. Just…keep talking.
        [*He leaves.*]
SALLY: You look awful.
MARTIN: I got up on the wrong side of the bed, perhaps.
SALLY: Not the wrong side of my bed.
MARTIN: No. I'd been drinking with Keith. Which is like…I was depressed.
SALLY: You were drunker than a skunk. You came round didn't you, and did your I'm not stopping routine. Where did you get that? It's eerie.
MARTIN: You heard me?
SALLY: Hard not to. Three choruses of *El Baniero Rosso* and then you threw a pineapple through the window. I have my reputation to think of. Give me your hand.
        [*She takes his hand and kisses it.*]
MARTIN: All right. I withdraw the singing, but not the pineapple.
SALLY: Why?
MARTIN: Because —
        [*He glances to the camera position and shields his lip movements.*]
        — because I wanted to get through to you, even with a not very large pineapple. I love you.
SALLY: Of course you don't.
MARTIN: I see.
SALLY: You don't.
MARTIN: I'm ashamed I disguise it so effectively, then. I don't want anything to do with this place but you. If he starts to turn over on that camera, I'm going to kill him. I hate him. I love you.
SALLY: You don't even hate him. And he likes you.
MARTIN: He does, does he?
SALLY: He says so.
MARTIN: When did he say that?
SALLY: Last night. He was there. He was trying to get me into bed, when a pineapple came through the window, thrown by a very gallant English gentleman.

MARTIN: Wait a minute. That bastard was with you last night?
SALLY: For a time. He'd come to ask me here today. The rest
was — well, sort of reflexive. I suppose he thought it
was expected of him. Which it was, of course. And
then the pineapple. We looked for you in the bushes for
a while, and then he left. Where did you end up?
MARTIN: The hotel. After quite a long walk. Sally —
SALLY: No, I'll talk. You can't make me the test of your happiness. It isn't fair. I bet you never even think the word,
most of the time. Happiness, I mean. I like you, and
I've started to dream about you, which, for reasons we
needn't go into, is such a relief. But I won't be a
touchstone to how you cope with this film. Who
started this Garden of Eden stuff?
MARTIN: It was something I started saying yesterday. You
could see Frank stick his hand out immediately, like a
falconer, waiting for the bloody words to come home
and roost. Sally, I can't just dust this off and walk
away and send you an anonymous card at Christmas.
SALLY: Oh, tish. I don't know anything about you, you don't
know a blind thing about me, it's ridiculous.
MARTIN: But it works like that.
SALLY: Sometimes.
MARTIN: Well. There you are.
SALLY: Sometimes.

> [*The noise of a wedding party has been coming closer.
> The music grows more and more wonderful.*]

MARTIN: Look, you could at least — I've been thinking, you
could fly home with me. For a holiday. For a week or
so, maybe not now, but…you could…
SALLY: I could what?
MARTIN: Later on this year?
SALLY: I could what?
MARTIN: Sally —

> [*The noise of the wedding is peaking.* FRANK *suddenly
> shouts.*]

FRANK: [*off*] Martin! Sally! Come on, snap out of it! Mehta's
got the wedding together. Martin — take her hand!

Just…not like that. Take her hand, put your arm round her if you like. It's a wedding. It's fixed for you to go and greet the old guy. *There,* for Christ's sake! The old guy with the white beard. Just hold hands and that's it. That's it. Enjoy!

[*Sudden blackout, as abruptly the music dies.*]

In the darkness, MEHTA*'s sad love song. When the lights go up, he is standing in* KEITH*'s hotel room. He is very quiet.*

KEITH: Well.

MEHTA: The sari is to your liking?

KEITH: Keep telling you, it's not for me.
[*He softens.*]
Lovely. Well. Want a drink?

MEHTA: [*holds up a hand*] I don't. You explain please.

KEITH: Go on then.

MEHTA: Frank has hired me for a week. But now is not requiring full services.

KEITH: Because you done so well. Forty six rolls. That was a bloody long wedding. That was an eight mag wedding. Has he said goodbye?

MEHTA: [*short*] Yes.

KEITH: Well, don't expect thanks. What'd he say?

MEHTA: He is giving my card to a friend.

KEITH: Hasn't got a bloody friend. Did you ever look at feet? Hot feet are the most obscene thing on the human body. No wonder they hate us. White people. I know you're not married, but you got any nephews or nieces?

MEHTA: Yes.

KEITH: Here we are then.
[*He gives him a tin of travel sweets.*]
Heathrow. And in here: medicines. Lomotil.

MEHTA: Lomotil?

KEITH: White man's medicine. He's paid you in full, hasn't he?

MEHTA: Oh yes.

KEITH: That's all it's about, mate. D'you get them finger-bells
           I asked you for?
                [MEHTA *rummages in his pocket. He passes them over.*]
           I could probably get 'em down the corner shop, but
           anyway...for *my* niece.
MEHTA: You are happy, Keith?
KEITH: It's against my religion to say. I'm shagged out.
MEHTA: You are religious man?
KEITH: I like a good funeral. Do you want to know how you
           done, Tourims? You done all right, pal. I've worked
           with worse.
                [*They look up.* MARTIN *enters.*]
MARTIN: Here you are. Frank tells me you're leaving us tomor-
           row.
KEITH: Tonight. He's off tonight.
MARTIN: Yes.
KEITH: I'll see you in the bar. Tata, Tourims.
                [*He holds out his hand.* MEHTA *takes it.* KEITH *leaves.*]
MARTIN: Well.
MEHTA: You enjoyed the wedding?
MARTIN: Very much. I like a good wedding.
MEHTA: The film is finished?
MARTIN: Another day. Mopping up. We leave on Friday. What
           is that?
MEHTA: Lomotil.
MARTIN: I should save it for a rainy day.
MEHTA: [*surprised*] A rainy day?
MARTIN: I hope you don't have any. That's ridiculously senti-
           mental: I wish you happiness, B.A., is what I'm trying
           to say.
MEHTA: [*bursts out*] Bloody shooting!
                [MARTIN *unstraps his watch.*]
MARTIN: Would you accept the present of my watch? It's —
           well, it's not new, obviously, but it is expensive —
           Swiss —
MEHTA: You think we have no watch in India? In India we
           have very good watch.

MARTIN: Of course, but I'd like you to have this one.
> [*For seconds it looks as though* MEHTA *might refuse.
> Then he snatches it, almost.*]

MEHTA: Well then, now I have been paid several times over. This bloody shooting is finished. I say goodbye, Martin. I have clients coming from Delhi, Festival of Goddess.

MARTIN: Must you hurry away now?
> [MEHTA *stares him in the eyes at last, as it were.*]

MEHTA: Shooting is finished.
> [*He leaves as* SALLY *comes on, elated. She does not recognise* MARTIN's *mood.*]

SALLY: Well, I thought you were just marvellous today. You were wonderful. All those old women loved you.

MARTIN: Frank's had enough. He's cut the schedule. We're going home the day after tomorrow.

SALLY: I know.

MARTIN: You know?

SALLY: He told me.

MARTIN: We're going to keep this up to the bitter end, are we? The old careless laughter?

SALLY: What careless laughter? I came to catch you before you started drinking and sinking. While you were still reasonably likely to ring the bell and wait for an answer. I've cooked for us. So if you're going to say you don't want to come back, don't go uprooting pineapples later.

MARTIN: I wouldn't even know where to start looking for a rotten pineapple if it was in the ground. The one I threw came from the kitchens here. I carried it a mile through the festering hellhole of a place you choose to live in.

SALLY: The Garden of Eden.

MARTIN: I want you to say you want me.

SALLY: I see.

MARTIN: I want an answer.

SALLY: You know how I got away from England? Came here? Bob was offered some work, of course. While he was thinking about it, I was getting knocked off by the manager of a wine-bar. At the time, the most important thing in the world was to have this wine-bar man ring up and have someone say 'Oh didn't you know? She doesn't live here any more.' And now...I like it here. I don't want to change.

MARTIN: [*sour*] Triff.

SALLY: It is. I never was anybody's, Martin, not really. I never will be. Do you want me to say what I really think has been happening, since I met you? It's pointless: there hasn't been the time.

MARTIN: Say it all the same.

SALLY: It's something you already know. You are intruders. Perhaps it would be different in a different place. It's the unedited us, this. It's the bit that ends up on the cutting room floor. Poor Martin. I'm giving you such a hard time. I'm not really as confident as I sound. Well, you already know that. When the lights are out, I mean.

MARTIN: I ought to have brained you with the bloody pineapple.

SALLY: Come home with me now. We can eat it.

MARTIN: Am I completely on the wrong foot?

SALLY: When?

[*A sudden blackout.*]

Abruptly, we are back in the cutting room and FRANK *and* CHRIS *are standing watching the screen on the Steenbeck, listening to the wedding music as the end credits roll. They are intent professionals.*

FRANK: Triff.

CHRIS: [*tallying with a Chinograph pencil*] What'd we say for the dog?

FRANK: You mean the dog sequence? Dog, gutters, blind beggar, crow, or vulture. Twenty.

CHRIS: Thirty.

FRANK: Go on then. What an ace ending. That music, man.

What a musician that old guy was. And the old
tabla…Ace. Ace-o.
> [*Enter* MARTIN.]

CHRIS: Fifty nine ten.

FRANK: Cracked it. *Cracked* it. Look at this, Martin! Just the
end, from where you trip on the step. Sensational.

CHRIS: What about Penny being in the shot?

FRANK: Fabulous.

CHRIS: What, with a stopwatch and clipboard?

FRANK: Verité, mate. Fabuloso.

MARTIN: It's clever.

FRANK: Clever? Wunderbar.

CHRIS: We can use that —

FRANK: Yeah! Where the — the —

CHRIS: Perfect, and then come back in…

FRANK: There! On a cut.

CHRIS: A mix, Frankie.

FRANK: No.
> [*He chops his palm for a cut.*]

CHRIS: You don't want to…like…come back to the smoke,
begin and end in the smoke, the mist, the magic —?

FRANK: [*allows*] Yeah. Go wide on the mountain, the music's
edged out, but —

CHRIS: It's still located, down there somewhere…

FRANK: And then…
> [CHRIS *fades the sound.* FRANK *turns to* MARTIN.]
What do you think?

MARTIN: Couldn't you take the credits in black…?

FRANK: Boring.

CHRIS: Take the credits over Martin's walkaway, his walk
through the paddy fields or whatever they are.

FRANK: No, man…You take the credits when the mood's hot.
There's the big close up of the bridegroom frowning,
then bing, bing, bing, bing, it's still happening, it's
good, we're happy, they're happy…Sensational. In
fact —

CHRIS: Take them even earlier!

FRANK: Exactly.

CHRIS: Great. What time is it? Listen, I'm going to go and get some Scotch from the office. What d'you say, Martin? A bloody great Scotch, feet up, get the wordies done?

MARTIN: I'll buy.

CHRIS: No you won't. I'll see you. Ten minutes.
[*He cuddles* FRANK.]
You bleeding old woman. It's great.

FRANK: [*primps*] I know.
[CHRIS *leaves.* MARTIN *and* FRANK *slump.*]

MARTIN: I hate it.

FRANK: You would.

MARTIN: It's beautiful, it's very cleverly edited, and I hate it.

FRANK: No you don't. You'll love it when it's dubbed. You've seen it with half the tracks missing, man. It'll work.

MARTIN: Perhaps it's me.

FRANK: It is Martin. It's vanity. Nobody likes to see themselves. It isn't you, on there; it can't be.

MARTIN: But it is you. Isn't it?

FRANK: You'll soon forget that when your poncey mates start saying how good it is. And don't give me any shit. If it wasn't any good that'd suit you even better. Your kind expect to be misrepresented; it's part of the lies; that it's all lies. If it isn't any good you'll go away and say, well, I went to India once with this frightful bugger making a film about God knows what. But it is. Good, I mean. Here.

MARTIN: What?

FRANK: It's a spliff.

MARTIN: I don't smoke that stuff.

FRANK: Well do. Victor Bleeding Ludorum.

MARTIN: You're an animal Frank.

FRANK: I am.

MARTIN: Well, say so.

FRANK: I'm an animal. Go on. Light up.

MARTIN: I don't feel that sociable.

FRANK: Who said anything about being sociable? It's a joint, man.

MARTIN: You want me to write the script stoned.

FRANK: I want you to write the script. Think what you can say.

MARTIN: Don't tempt me. I've been dreaming of beating you to a squibbering pulp.

FRANK: What kind of a pulp?

MARTIN: The word was squibbering.

FRANK: Well, you learn something new every day.

MARTIN: The day you learn something new, Frank — listen, would you ever go back?

FRANK: Did I leave something behind?

[*Sudden blackout.*]

THE END

Also available from Amber Lane Press:

Julian Mitchell   FRANCIS

Francis of Assisi was a man totally dedicated to a missionary life of poverty and simplicity. He wished to follow the gospels literally and to be a true disciple of Christ. In this play Julian Mitchell writes about the forces that turned Brother Francis into Saint Francis.

Julian Mitchell   ANOTHER COUNTRY

One of the West End's resounding successes of 1982, winning the SWET award for 'Play of the Year'. The setting is an English public school in the 1930's. The two central characters, Guy Bennett and Tommy Judd, are both, in their own different ways, rebels and outsiders who dare to fight against the system.

Hugh Whitemore   PACK OF LIES

Based on the real events surrounding an American couple living in Britain, Helen and Peter Kroger, who were found guilty of spying for the Russians in 1961. The action centres around the Jackson family who as friends and neighbours of the Krogers are drawn into a conspiracy of betrayal. A West End play starring Judi Dench and Michael Williams.

Ronald Harwood   THE DRESSER

Michael Billington found *The Dresser* '...a wonderfully affectionate and intelligent play about the theatre. It captures not only the equivocal relationship between star and dresser, it also conveys the bitchiness, the sentiment, the anecdotage, plus the feeling that the backstage world is itself a little kingdom, a tatty Camelot worshipping a prop Holy Grail.' Released as a feature film in 1984, starring Albert Finney and Tom Courtenay.

For a complete catalogue of our plays write or telephone:
Amber Lane Press, 9 Middle Way, Oxford OX2 7LH.
Tel. Oxford 50545